# Who to blame

## Direct your lawsuits at

Contributors
James Schloeffel
Charles Firth
Cam Smith
Gregor Stronach
Ben Keating

Print Editor
Cam Smith

Shovel Editor
James Schloeffel

Editor-at-Large
Charles Firth

## Subscriptions

Subscriptions - The Chaser
chasershop.com
subscriptions@chaser.com.au
Phone: 02 8227 6486

Memberships - The Shovel
theshovel.com.au/membership

## Image Credits

The following images are licenced under Creative Commons 3.0/4.0

Scott Morrison (pgs 5, 7, 35): Commonwealth of Australia 2016



The Chaser Quarterly

The Chaser's Disclaimer Managing editor: Charles Firth. This is the fifteenth issue of **The Chaser Quarterly**, and is published by Chaser Quarterly Pty Ltd (ACN 141758812) of 27/57 Hereford St, Glebe, NSW, 2037. While effort has been made to verify any facts contained within this publication, no responsibility will be taken for errors or omissions contained herein by Chaser Quarterly Pty Ltd, its officers, employees or their agents. Readers should rely on their own enquiries when making decisions touching on their interests. Apart from satirical articles which discuss public figures for the purposes of humour, any mention of any person, alive or dead, is entirely coincidental. We expect readers to use their own common sense in determining the truth or otherwise of any statement in this publication. **The Chaser Quarterly** is available in bookshops across Australia, and is printed by Spotpress, 24-26 Lilian Fowler Pl, Marrickville, NSW, 2204. Subscribe at **chasershop.com** and stay up to date at **chaser.com.au**

# WELCOME TO THE SHOVEL AND THE CHASER QUARTERLY'S OFFICIAL ELECTION GUIDEBOOK FOR THE AUSTRALIAN FEDERAL ELECTION 2019 FIRST EDITION PART 1

Yes, we should probably have workshopped a snappier title, but in our defence, we've only had three years to prepare for this.

Now you may rightfully ask, "*How can you legally call this the 'official' election guide? Isn't that illegal?*" Well dear reader, unlike the idiots at the AEC, a certain pair of satiric publishing organisations thought ahead for this election and registered "The Official" as a 100% government-recognised trademark, so from now on if anyone wants to call anything Official, they're going to have to go through us.

Sure, some of you legal eagles may say, "*Hey, wait a second, that's not how trademarks work!*", but to those people we say, we've also registered "that's not how trademarks work" as a trademark, so now you owe us money.

This year marks 18 years since The Chaser first hit the airwaves with The Election Chaser, and 7 years since the Shovel hit the World Wide Web, and we like to think democracy has improved in leaps and bounds since those early days. In fact, we've been so successful fixing democracy that there is no longer any need for satirical television shows about the election.

Yes, no longer do politicians lie, cheat, or steal. No longer are we subject to elections centred on fibs about boats. And I think it's safe to say our allies the UK and America have never been more democratically sound.

Anyway my Uber is here, so if you could type all that up Janette, and maybe come up with a closing paragraph, that'd be great.

Charles Firth
*As dictated*

# LETTERS *to the* EDITOR

Dear Editor,

Regarding my opinion piece in the last issue ('***Why gays can't be trusted with something as sacrosanct as marriage***'), I'd like to clarify a few comments that I made.

When I wrote that "marriage is not just something you throw away as soon as a better piece of sauce comes along", I meant it purely in relation to the way homosexuals might treat marriage. Obviously, when a red-blooded straight man finds a better piece of sauce, then it's a completely different matter.

When I said "it's disgusting how some people flaunt their personal relationships across our television screens and tabloids, shoving it in our face," I meant it entirely in relation to gay relationships. I won't go into it here why, but you can catch my full explanation for why gays talking about their relationship is so problematic on my latest tell-all interview on Sunday Night on Channel Seven.

When I said that it's important that "kids get brought up by their biological parents", obviously there is the exception when a father has a very good reason to leave the family unit, for example, to look after his other family unit that he created on the side with the better piece of sauce.
I'm sick and tired of gays and lesbians trashing the institution of marriage. It's something that should be left to straight people to do.

Barnaby Joyce
Armadale, NSW

---

Dear Editor,

There has been a lot of media interest in the $2700 holiday that I took from HelloWorld at the same time they were tendering for a lucrative contract from my department. I am as appalled as the public that this happened. Clearly there needs to be some sort of watchdog set up that can thoroughly investigate how this sort of information came to be known to the media.

Matthias Cormann
Singapore

---

Dear Editor,

By the way, you didn't hear it from me, but it's probably worth looking into Peter Dutton's links to a company called Paladin.

M. Turnbull
Point Piper, NSW

---

Dear Editor,

I take exception to all the corruption scandals dominating the

## Did you know?

The word 'Democracy' comes from the Greek word *demokratia* which means "to decide between two terrible options."

news cycle in the run up to the 2019 Federal Election. Why can't it be like the old days, when elections were all about race-baiting and refugee bashing.

Pauline Hanson
Ipswich, QLD

---

Dear Editor,

There has been a lot of speculation in recent weeks about how I came to be a millionaire during the decade that I was a Queensland police officer earning a salary of $75,000. Clearly there needs to be a watchdog set up to thoroughly investigate where this speculation is coming from and stamp it out.

Peter Dutton
Investment Property Number 5, QLD

---

Dear Editor,

I found your article about me in the last issue most amusing ("The 10 Ways Bill Shorten Could Lose the Next Election"). The writer clearly doesn't know what they're talking about. The idea that there are only ten ways in which I'll squander my unassailable lead is nonsense. I can think of hundreds.

Bill Shorten
Moonee Ponds, VIC

---

Dear Editor,

It now seems inevitable that some sort of federal anti-corruption commission will need to be set up. Personally I blame Labor. If they hadn't lost the 2013 election, then none of these corruption scandals would be happening.
And anyway, it's completely unnecessary. My front bench don't need a watchdog to help them out with corruption. They can do it themselves.

Nevertheless, I have to look like I'm doing something. Therefore, I'd like to announce the establishment of a tendering process to find a private company to run the independent commission against corruption. I've invited Helloworld to tender for it. And to make sure the tender process is run with the highest integrity, I'm making the entire Liberal Party frontbench leave the country while it is carried out, so that nobody can accuse us of influencing the outcome. We'll be in Singapore.

Scott Morrison
The Shire, NSW

---

**CORRECTION**

The editors would like to apologise for the fact that the Prime Minister is erroneously referred to as Scott Morrison in multiple places throughout this publication. We can only assume that since going to print, the role of Prime Minister has changed at least three times. If you would like to correct these mistakes, simply send $3 in a sealed envelope C/O 'Why the fuck is Chris Pyne* Prime Minister' and we will mail you out some whiteout and a non-permanent marker to make the relevant corrections.

*Sorry, this should now be 'Why the fuck is Greg Hunt Prime Minister'.

## ✉ Do you have a letter for the editor?

Well it's too late now isn't it? This book went to print weeks ago, so you should have got your act together sooner.

# A PERSONAL MESSAGE FROM SCOTT MORRISON

G'day,

Scott Morrison here, your new PM. I'm getting in touch today because I want to tell you something really important. And that's that I'm a regular, everyday, ordinary, average, fair dinkum, dinky di, down-to-earth, true blue Aussie bloke on $400k a year, just like you.

In a moment, I'm going to tell you that I'm getting on with the job. But first, a bit about me. My Mum calls me Scott, but my focus group-tested nickname is ScoMo. Do you know any other 50 year-old men who refer to themselves by their nickname? Apparently it's a deadset normal thing to do. Go Sharks.

Right now I'm travelling around Australia on a big bus talking to regular Aussies. 'Bus' of course is the term ordinary Aussie mums and dads use for VIP jets. And my VIP jet is about as fair dinkum Aussie as they come. Not like those VIP jets in the Canberra bubble.

As I've been travelling around this great country, a lot of people have come up to me in the street and said, "ScoMo, you're just an average Aussie bloke who likes a beer and understands the unique pressures of life in middle class Australia in 2019". Actually that may have been the briefing notes I put together for my image management firm. My mistake. But the point I want to make is that I walk in streets just like you. I had a beer in a street once.

I said before that I was going to tell you how I'm getting on with the job. Well, it's simple. I'm travelling around the country putting in the hard yards, rolling up my sleeves, getting my hands dirty, getting down to business, trucking ahead, head down, bum up, getting on with things, having a crack, and getting on with having a genuine Aussie go at getting the job done. That's how. It's not rocket science when you think about it. Electricity prices.

So next time you see me around, come up and say g'day. I'll be the guy wearing the cap that 57% of focus group participants said makes me seem more natural and approachable.

Hooroo.
ScoMo

# HOW THE SEATS COULD FALL

The House of Representatives is made up of 150 people from right across the country. As the name suggests, it is a totally representative sample of the nation's former lawyers, political staffers, union bosses and Bob Katter.

Within these main groupings there are factions, sub-factions, fractions and Bob Katter. Each member gets one go at being Prime Minister.

The members are organised into parties – the former lawyers and political staffers on one side, the former union bosses and other political staffers on the other. Bob Katter sits in the middle and provides an articulate running commentary of events.

To achieve government this time around, the former political staffers and union bosses must unseat at least one former lawyer or political staffer. Whoever wins the majority of seats gets to form government and appoint a Royal Commission of their choice.

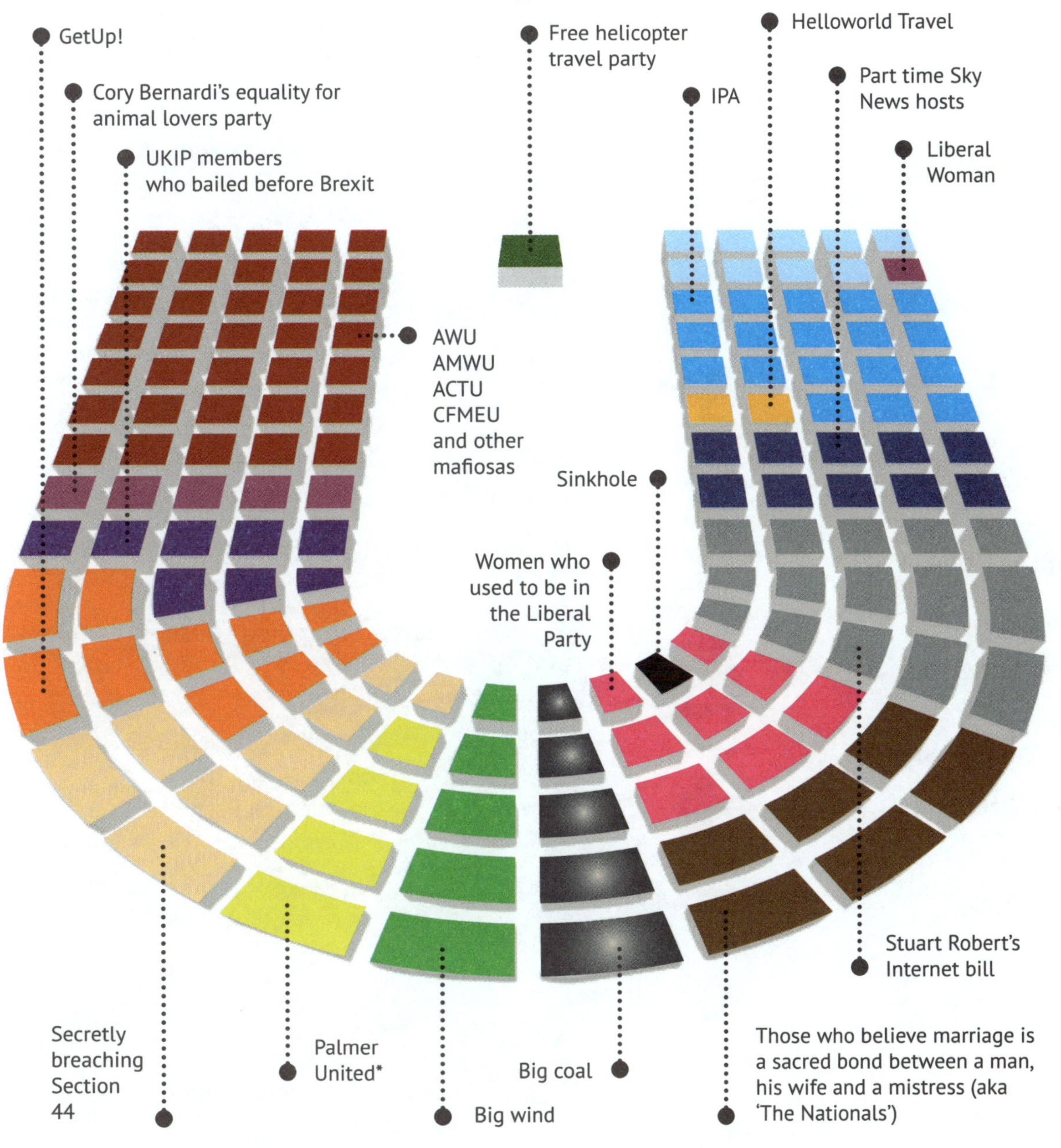


* In the loose sense of the word

# HEAD TO HEAD

## The Leaders On The Key Issues

| CANDIDATE | **Scott Morrison**<br>Liberal |
|---|---|
| ENERGY | Says that under a Coalition Government 90% of Australia's electricity will be powered by Fair Dinkum Energy, whatever the fuck that means. |
| BUSINESS | If you have a go you get a go. If you have a multinational business you get a tax-free status. |
| SAME-SEX MARRIAGE | Believes marriage is between a man and the right-wing of his political party. |
| INNOVATION | Believes he is the right man to lead Australia into the 1970s |
| PUBLIC TRANSPORT | Stopped the boats, much to the anger of Manly commuters. |
| IMMIGRATION | Says he will further strengthen Australia's border policies, vowing to blow up any boat that enters Australian waters. |
| FOREIGN AFFAIRS | Says affairs with foreigners are the responsibility of the National Party |
| HOUSING | 6. |
| EDUCATION | Wants to give more children the opportunity to learn that the Earth was created 4,000 years ago. |
| CLIMATE CHANGE | Agrees with the 97% of News Corp columnists who say climate change isn't real. |

| | **Bill Shorten**<br>Labor | **That Other Guy**<br>Australian Greens |
|---|---|---|
| | Sucks it out of a room | Is afraid of power, which is why he joined The Greens. |
| | Once had a friend who knew someone who worked in the private sector for a while. | Says The Greens started disrupting profitable industries way before it became fashionable. |
| | Believes in the sanctity of all unions. | As Australia's most progressive party, the Greens believe every Australian should take part in an archaic religious ritual. |
| | Wore double denim to a friend's party last year. | Believes every product can be made from hemp if we put our minds to it. |
| | Catches the bus to work every day, you just never notice him. | Will triple the number of yellow bikes dumped on the side of the road by 2050. |
| | Says he will further strengthen Australia's border policies, vowing to blow up any boat that enters Australian waters – but in a compassionate way. | Borders are a state of mind. |
| | Kept his affair local. | Would like to have an affair with the entire Swedish system of government. |
| | 3. | Hopes every Australian home will run off a $500,000 solar battery by 2020. |
| | Believes every Australian should be able to go to a school totally unlike the one he went to. | Believes every Australian school child should run off five $500,000 batteries by 2020. |
| | Has solemnly pledged that there will be no carbon tax under a government he leads - so there almost certainly will be one. | Notes that the Greens' opposition to the ETS in 2010 reduced Kevin Rudd's emissions by 100%. |

60 Seconds With...

# Barnaby Joyce MP

**Q: How are you Barnaby?**
A: I don't want to talk about my family.

**Q: I didn't ask you about your family.**
A: The fact that Vicki and I haven't had sex since January is none of your business.

**Q: Shall we do this another time?**
A: Like I said, my son's developmental issues are not something that need to be splashed around in the media.

**Q: I think we'll end it there.**
A: I fucked another staffer.

*image: Simon.chamberlain / Wikipedia*

## THIS ELECTION TAKE A SHITBET. THE FIRST $50 YOU WASTE IS ON US.

**ELECTION NIGHT ODDS ★ ★ ★**

| | |
|---|---|
| Scott Morrison blames Labor for the Coalition's defeat | $1.80 |
| Labor Party wins, then immediately fucks it up | $1.01 |
| Antony Green gets a stiffy while explaining how the senate voting system works | $2.25 |
| Peta Credlin tells Sky News that the Liberal Party was better when she was leader | $5.00 |
| Leigh Sales tongue-pashes Malcolm Turnbull | $8.00 |
| Bill Shorten runs out of batteries before getting to the end of his victory speech | $4.80 |
| Shorten drops his cue-cards and adlibs by asking the audience what their favourite lettuce is | $0.20 |
| Tim Wilson offers to fill out ballots for voters at polling booths | $1.60 |
| Bill Shorten announced winner by 9pm. Anthony Albanese calls for a spill by 10pm | $0.02 |
| Peter Dutton blames Coalition loss on refugee advocates | $3.25 |
| New One Nation candidate wins a senate seat then immediately quits the party | $2.40 |
| Andrew Wilkie takes this bet | $10,000 |
| Cory Bernardi accidentally thanks his dog instead of his wife during his victory speech | $3.50 |

*To place a bet, simply select your betting option, and then place the amount you wish to bet into the nearest bin.*

***Just like other betting companies, but faster.***

# HOW THE MEDIA COVERED THE ISSUES

## Morrison VS Shorten

THE AUSTRALIAN

Morrison consolidates Newspoll lead in "Most Preferred PM Named Scott"

The Sydney Morning Herald

Morrison plummets in poll almost as much as Sydney's house prices have

Daily Mail

Home | TV&Showbiz | Femail | Health | Science | Weather

Royal Family | Breaking News | Sydney | Melbourne | Brisbane | Perth |

Bill Shorten is spending up to 30 HOURS A DAY at his ex-wife's gym in preparation for his debate with Scott Morrison

theguardian

Greens surge to 8% in latest poll: Di Natale open to forming government

MAMAMIA NEWS ENTERTAINMENT LIFESTYLE PARENTING BEAUTY & STY

This Bill Shorten versus Scott Morrison 'Love Actually' spoof actually made us tear up

## The Great Barrier Reef

theguardian

A Generation's Shame: We're not just destroying the reef, we're destroying our future

FINANCIAL REVIEW

'Too late to save the Reef': Adani shares jump

THE AUSTRALIAN

News in brief: Reef gets brighter

MAMAMIA NEWS ENTERTAINMENT LIFESTYLE PARENTING BEAUTY & STYLE HEALTH RELATIONSHIPS VIDEO

Why the Great Barrier Reef is the perfect place to have your affair

change.org Start a petition

Sign this petition to stop coral bleaching in Queensland and also this other petition to increase car parking spaces in Indiana

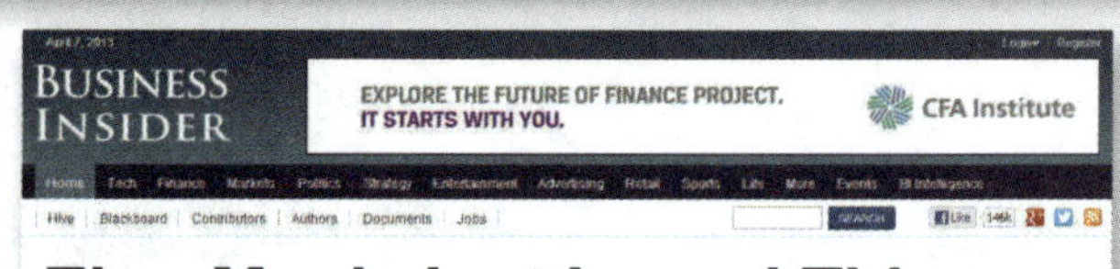


Elon Musk Just Issued This Warning About Coral Bleaching

## Negative Gearing

**The Sydney Morning Herald**

Housing price plunge stokes hopes that Shorten will change tack on negative gearing

**BUSINESS INSIDER**

What Elon Musk thinks about Negative Gearing

**Crikey**

What does Morrison's stance on negative gearing say about his weird religious beliefs?

**THE AUSTRALIAN**

Labor's stance on Negative Gearing proves that George Pell is innocent

This couple bought a house completely on their own with only a small $2 million loan from their parents, now Labor wants to kill them

**Daily Mail**

WATCH: MAFS star tries to explain how to buy a house, and while he's doing that, his WIFE ducks off to have an affair IN THE NEXT ROOM

**MAMAMIA**

I had an affair with someone who was negative gearing, and it was heart breaking but tax effective

**THE CONVERSATION**

Negative gearing has benefits and costs and Morrison should do something or nothing or both

## Healthcare

**THE AUSTRALIAN**

Hospital funding in crisis: cuts inevitable

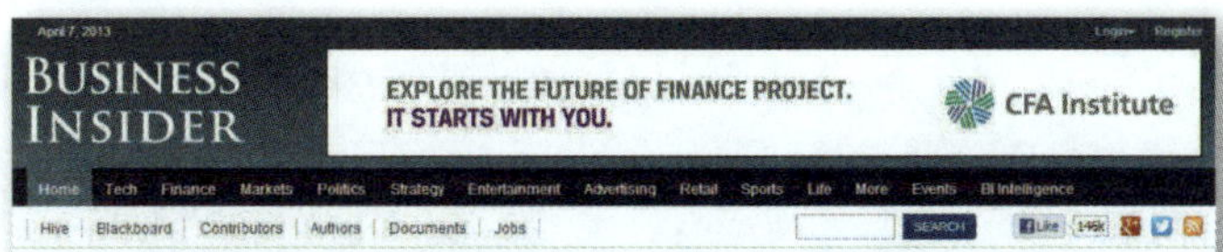


Your 10-second guide to what Elon Musk thinks of hospital funding in Australia

**MAMAMIA**

How regular masturbation could save our health system billions

**THE AGE**

Hospital funding in crisis: tax increases inevitable

**theguardian**

Why your latest Medicare refund should make you feel guilty

He thought it was just a freckle, but then he found out what it really was, and it almost killed him

## Opinion

# Herald Sun

# THERE IS NO RIGHT CHOICE THIS ELECTION

BY **ANDREW BOLT**

In this election, Australia has a choice. Between the guy who replaced the guy who replaced Tony Abbott, and the guy who wants to replace the guy who replaced the guy who replaced Tony Abbott. But the choice is easy. Tony Abbott. Should still be Prime Minister. Tony Abbott.

So what you do is you take your ballot. Draw a diagonal line across it. And write Tony Abbott. In big letters. As big as the man's heart.

Is it a crime for me to tell you to spoil your ballot? Maybe it is. But it's a crime to cut down the best prime minister we've ever had. And Malcolm Turnbull walks free.

Like free enterprise. Like the freedom to write whatever you like about Aborigines or non-Aborigines or whatever I want to call them. Freedom is good, unless it's the freedom to call a leadership challenge just because you have the numbers.

Which was a good idea when Malcolm Turnbull was leader. It's complicated. But you know who isn't? I know who isn't. I know him well, because we often share a meal. Tony Abbott.

Imagine your house is on fire. Then the doorbell rings, and it's a politician at the door. Which politician would you want it to be? Tony Abbott. He'd pitch in. Wouldn't want any cameras, and would say so on camera. Until there was a good take. Just get the job done. Tony Abbott.

And if your house was in the Davidson RFS district, that's who you'd get. Tony Abbott. In a yellow fireproof suit. Because he shows up.

His wife wanted him to retire, you know. So did all three daughters. But he didn't listen. He was Minister for Women, he knows what's best for them. Tony Abbott. Shows up even when not wanted.

He kept going. Even though polls showed that most voters in Warringah thought it was time to retire. He doesn't retire. That's not what Tony Abbott does. Even if it jeopardises the party's chances. He's a selfless guy, Tony Abbott is. Serves his country. Even when that means serving himself.

What if it isn't your house that's burning, but Australia's burning? With the flames of a budget emergency. Also literally burning because of climate change some would have you believe but they're wrong. I know and Tony Abbott knows.

Who else can solve the budget emergency? Not Labor. They created such a big emergency that Tony Abbott had to raise the debt ceiling just to solve it. And even though he knew he'd get criticised for it, called a hypocrite because the deficit blew out even further on his watch, he did it anyway, because that's the kind of guy he is. It's called being a good bloke. The best bloke. Tony Abbott.

Australia, you made a big mistake with this one. It breaks my heart. But mark my words, it will break yours, too. Literally break it in two when ISIS come for you, or that madman Vladimir Putin, because the only one strong enough to stand up to them is Tony Abbott.

This year Australia will face a choice. Not the right choice, because it's not a choice involving Tony Abbott. But in a way, it still is, if I want it to be. Which I do. You know who to choose, Australia. Tony Abbott.

Daily Mail.com

**An investigative report into why the fuck all our headlines are so long and why every one seems to have three celebrity name drops and eight unrelated sentences in them.**

**MAFS Kylie Jenner I'm a Celebrity Get Me Out Of Here Prince Harry Sophie Monk Andy Lee Karl Stephanovic Kyle Sandilands, there that should sort us out for an entire month.**

# There is no correct choice this election

**115** shares

BY **STAFF WRITER**

In this election, the country has a choice. Between the guy who replaced the guy who replaced Tony Abbott, and the guy who wants to replace the guy who replaced the guy who replaced Tony Abbott. But the choice is easy. Tony Abbott. Should still be Prime Minister. Tony Abbott.

So what you do is you take your ballot. Draw a diagonal line across it. And write Tony Abbott. In big letters. As big as the man's heart.

Is it a crime for me to tell you to spoil your ballot? Maybe it is. But it's a crime to cut down the best prime minister we've ever had. And Malcolm Turnbull walks free.

Like free enterprise. Like the freedom to write whatever you like about Aborigines or non-Aborigines or whatever I want to call them. Freedom is good, unless it's the freedom to call a leadership challenge just because you have the numbers.

Which was a good idea when Malcolm Turnbull was leader. It's complicated. But you know who isn't? I know who isn't. I know him well, because we often share a meal. Tony Abbott.

Imagine your house is on fire. Then the doorbell rings, and it's a politician at the door. Which politician would you want it to be? Tony Abbott. He'd pitch in. Wouldn't want any cameras, and would say so on camera. Until there was a good take. Just get the job done. Tony Abbott.

And if your house was in the Davidson RFS district, that's who you'd get. Tony Abbott. In a yellow fireproof suit. Because he shows up.

His wife wanted him to retire, you know. So did all three daughters. But he didn't listen. He was Minister for Women, he knows what's best for them. Tony Abbott. Shows up even when not wanted.

He kept going. Even though polls showed that most voters in Warringah thought it was time to retire. He doesn't retire. That's not what Tony Abbott does. Even if it jeopardises the party's chances. He's a selfless guy, Tony Abbott is. Serves his country. Even when that means serving himself.

What if it isn't your house that's burning, but Australia's burning? With the flames of a budget emergency. Also literally burning because of climate change some would have you believe but they're wrong. I know and Tony Abbott knows.

Who else can solve the budget emergency? Not Labor. They created such a big emergency that Tony Abbott had to raise the debt ceiling just to solve it. And even though he knew he'd get criticised for it, called a hypocrite because the deficit blew out even further on his watch, he did it anyway, because that's the kind of guy he is. It's called being a good bloke. The best bloke. Tony Abbott.

Australia, you made a big mistake with this one. It breaks my heart. But mark my words, it will break yours, too. Literally break it in two when ISIS come for you, or that madman Vladimir Putin, because the only one strong enough to stand up to them is Tony Abbott.

This year Australia will face a choice. Not the right choice, because it's not a choice involving Tony Abbott. But in a way, it still is, if I want it to be. Which I do. You know who to choose, Australia. Tony Abbott.

# Opinion

# theguardian

## It's time to face facts. There's no such thing as an ethical guacamole dip for your election night party

**Guardian Staff Writer**

I was the first person in my family to go to university or buy an avocado. So I understand first hand the complicated ethical-political dilemma facing Australians when they consider whether or not to make a Mexican-inspired accoutrement for their election-night guests.

Putting aside the highly gendered symbolism of a woman making anything at all, one is left with the simple fact that we have – or should have – moved beyond the need to mix avocado, onion and lemon into an unnecessary, albeit tasty, chunky dip.

For starters, how can you be sure where your avocado came from? And even if you do know, what if your taste for chili – which is increasingly being added to guacamole these days – is having an unintended effect on the native animal populations of northern Asia. We just don't know.

Of course in an election year, guacamole becomes even more problematic. As Donald Trump incites fear about Mexicans 'flooding' across the border into the United States, is your pseudo-Mexican dish simply adding to the angst that these desperate people must be feeling? Or is it, in fact, a statement of solidarity? If dipping a corn chip into guacamole can make us focus our attention on the plight of asylum seekers – one could argue – maybe it's worth the extra food miles required to access the ingredients.

I'm not convinced. As is so often the case with popular commoditised dips and nibbles, while the benefits are clear, the true costs are impossible to measure. Best to be on the side and not throw an election party at all.

**This is The Guardian's model for open, independent journalism**

**Our mission is to keep on making this fucking yellow box at the bottom of your screen bigger and bigger until it gets to the point that the only place you can click is the 'donate' button. Think you can just read around it? Go on, try your best, eventually you're just going to be so frustrated you'll empty your entire wallet into an envelope and mail it to us just to get this damned thing out of your face. Let's be honest though, it's still a million times less irritating than anything Miranda Devine has ever written.**

[ When the picnic special of MAFS is going to reveal a bombshell twist ]

You deserve to know.

The Sydney Morning Herald

YOU CAN HARDLY TELL WE'RE NOW OWNED BY NINE

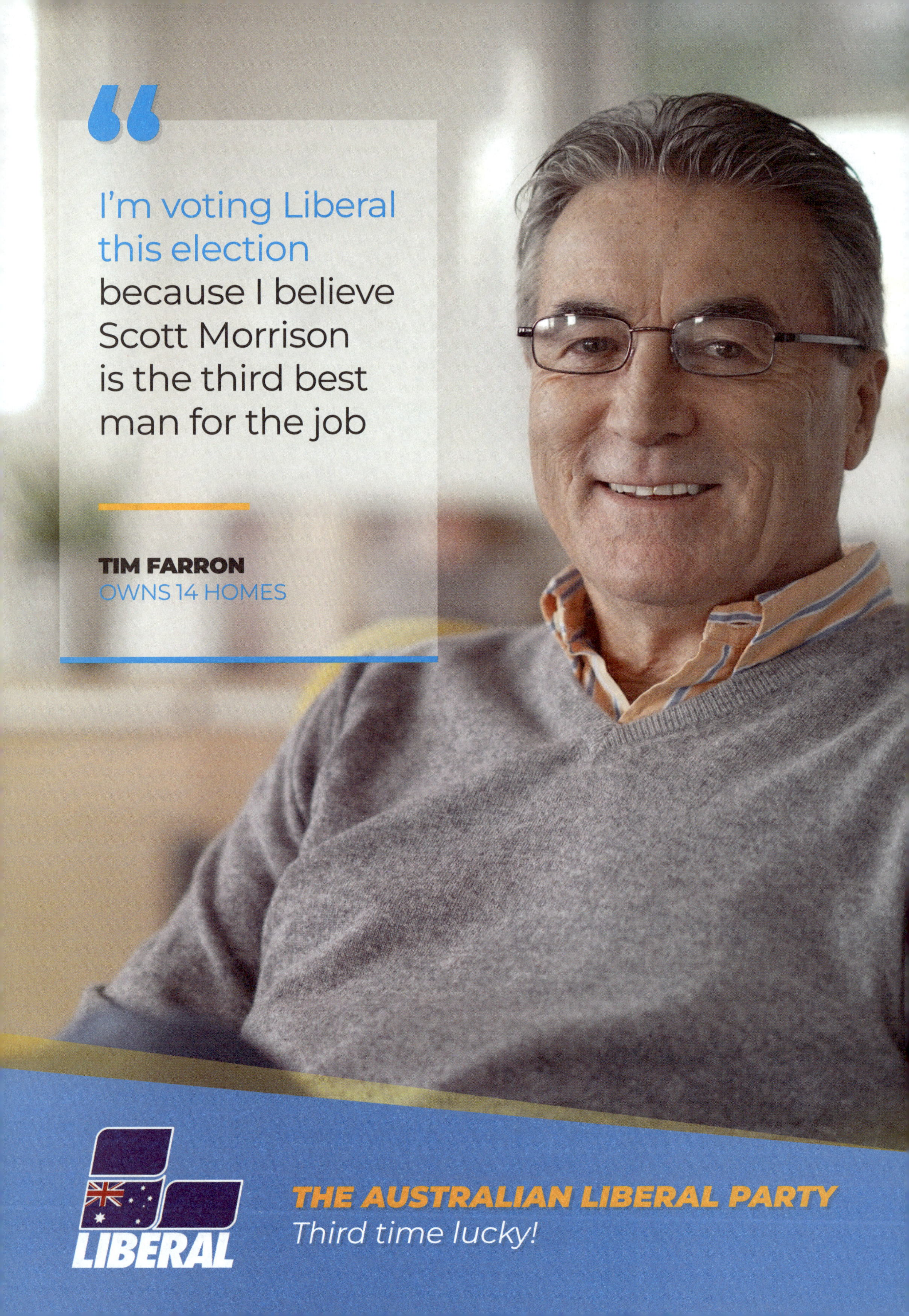

“

I’m voting Liberal this election because I believe Scott Morrison is the third best man for the job

**TIM FARRON**
OWNS 14 HOMES

**THE AUSTRALIAN LIBERAL PARTY**
*Third time lucky!*

THE CONVERSATION Australia's favourite all natural sedative

# To Australia's shame, the NBN lags behind the rest of the world

by **Michelle Grattan AO**

When Malcolm Turnbull promised, at the 2013 election, to fix Labor's NBN roll-out (and slice $20 billion off the cost of delivery) he created for himself more headaches than he solved.

Under Turnbull, instead of cabling fibre optic wire into everyone's homes, the NBN leaves the 'final mile' of internet delivery on the ancient copper network.

Turnbull sold his fix as being cheaper to deliver and faster to build, but the result is that Australia is ranked just 49th in the world when it comes to internet download speeds.

To give some sense of international comparison, that means an average Australian, attempting to download an HD version of Two Girls, One Cup would only reach the point where the girl poos into the cup in the time that it takes the average Singaporean to download the whole thing.

Even in Russia, the download would have got to the point where the girls are tastily licking the poo in the cup, while in the USA, in the same amount of time, the download would be past the licking scene and all the way up to the point where the other girl is sticking her fingers down her throat and vomiting into the cup.

It says something about Malcolm Turnbull's priorities that, by the time the average Australian can get to the scene where they're eating the poo-vomit out of the cup, the average South Korean has downloaded two-and-a-half copies of the full HD video, complete with commentary track.

But the real story is not just in download speeds, it's also in upload speeds – which is key in a world that is increasingly reliant upon User Generated Content (UGC). By 2025, the average Australian, wanting to upload their own scat videos to the internet will have to wait 16 times as long as the average Swede.

Many young Australians, voting for the first time, will be keenly aware of the lag required to download Two Girls, One Cup. As we head to the polls this election, the Coalition needs a more convincing response to fix this urgent and growing problem.

*Michelle Grattan is Chief Political Correspondent at The Conversation*

# Opinion

ABC NEWS

Mosman Library / Flickr

# Hey Ho! This Election Really Takes The Cake!

By Annabel Crabb

Pop the champers and ice your lemon tarts, it's election time again! Can I get a whoop whoop? No, ok fair enough.

Still, you have to admit it's wonderful. That magical time once every three years (two and a half when we're extra good), when us policy wonks get our collective knickers in a proverbial knot. Bring out the lightly salted popcorn, I say – let's get this show on the road.

Who's going to win? Will it be Scott 'Sponge Cake' Morrison. Or Bill 'Shortbread' Shorten? Impossible to say. If you've come for a serious analysis, you've come to the wrong column. Try Michelle Grattan.

But if you want to hear me compare each of the 300 major party candidates to a baked dessert item, read on comrade. Read on.

Barnaby Joyce? A pineapple upside-down cake – bronzed, crumbly, and just a little bit weird. Tony Abbott, the dark chocolate torte – extra bitter with an aftertaste that will punch you in the face. I could go on.

And I will. Eric Abetz, a chocolate soufflé – serious and really fucking difficult. Albo? The strudel, obviously.

Delicious! But not quite as delicious as my next segue. Sausage sizzles.

If the Fraser-Hawke-Keating-Howard-Rudd-Gillard-Rudd-Abbott-Turnbull-Morrison years have taught us anything, it's that Australians love a good election-day fry up. As any self-respecting tong-twirler will tell you, it's the highlight of election day.

Still, it pays to have a sausage sizzle plan of attack. Without one, you'll be on a one-way express train to Troublesville (without the infrastructure funding required to build the track to get back home).

The secret? Skip the how-to-vote-cards (they're as predictable as a sponge cake in Eden Monaro), get the voting out of the way, then hit up the sausages. And then head on home to hit the booze. Because if there's one thing I've learnt from election nights, it's that getting smashed quicker than an Italian marble table at a Tony Abbott leaving do is the only way to numb the boredom.

Cake reference.

# KITCHEN CABINET

## *With Annabel Crabb*

*Join journalist Annabel Crabb and Cambodian dictator Pol Pot on ABC1 this Saturday for a lighthearted chat about cookies, cakes and what it's like juggling three kids while trying to cover up a genocide.*

# Barnaby Joyce Paternity Tests

**100% FAILURE RATE GUARANTEE**

**IT'S SIMPLE!**

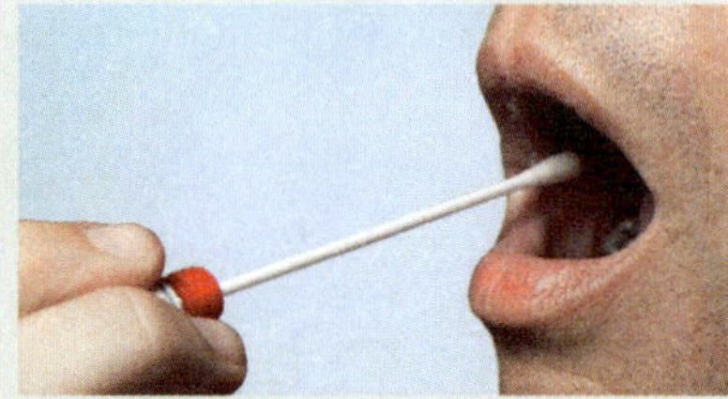

STEP 1

STEP 2

STEP 3

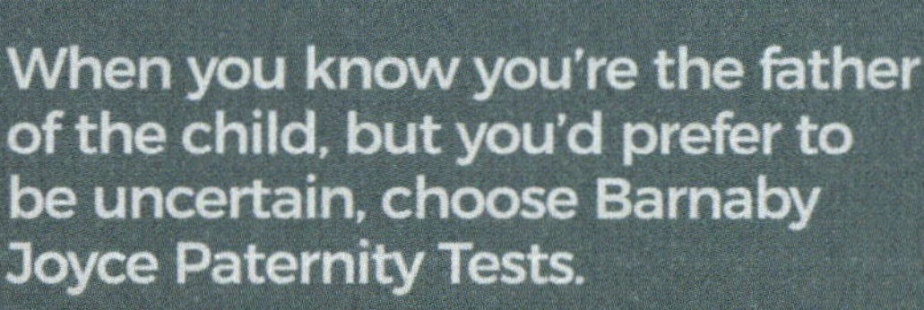

sky NEWS

# This Chaos Never Would Have Happened When I Was PM

Peta Credlin, *Sky News*

The Coalition is heading for a humiliating defeat and they only have themselves to blame. The sloppiness, the infighting, the scandals. None of these things would have happened in my years as Prime Minister.

Do these people even know how to run a campaign? I don't think so. We've got backbenchers contradicting one another, ministers not being able to articulate policies. Who's in charge here? Who's the campaign manager? When I was Prime Minister, I had the best campaign manager. Me.

Of course, we all know why we're in such a dire state now. Malcolm Bligh Turnbull. Since he overthrew me to take the top job, things have become an absolute debacle.

Some saw Turnbull as the Messiah. But I knew how this would play out. He's all show and no substance. Doesn't have the guts or the grunt to succeed under the pressure of a campaign like I did. Doesn't have a Chief of Staff like I did either (P. Credlin).

Inexplicably, he pushed the Liberal Party towards the scary centre. If the Victorian election taught us anything, it's that people want the Liberal Party to be more right wing.

But worst of all, he created yet further instability by being torn down as leader. How selfish.

I don't mind Scott Morrison. But the damage has been done. Don't be surprised if the party asks me to put my hand up for the leadership again. They're only human.

# Australia's Electoral Contract

## AGREEMENT

**PARTIES**

Scott Morrison

**and**

Bill Shorten

**and**

Australian Voters

**RECITALS**

A The Parties acknowledge that the office of the Prime Minister must be pursued with honesty and vigour.

B The Parties recognise that the Australian Voters are smart, discerning citizens.

C Notwithstanding any of the previous recitals, the Parties recognise that the democratic process peaked around the time of *Australian Idol Season 3,* and even that was a pretty shit result.

**DEFINITION**

'*Election*' is defined as any event where participation ensures access to a sausage sizzle; save and except for any such sizzle which occurs within 10 metres of the entrance to a Bunnings store (for such instances, see s 4 of the *Bunnings & Miscellaneous Fairs (School and Church) Act 1974 (Cth)*). Any such sausage sizzle may also offer cans of drink, so long as the price of said cans does not exceed the higher of:

(a) $1.00 AUD; or

(b) half the cost of the sausage.

'*Election Issue*' is defined as something that affects the hard working mums and dads in Sydney's western suburbs.

'*Cost of living pressures*' means the pressure to add the *Sports Bundle* to your Foxtel monthly contract.

'*The greatest moral, social and economic challenge of our time*' means an issue that did well in focus groups for a while, that we exploited to get elected.

'*Prime Minister*' was originally defined as a statesman/woman of singular talent, but then Kevin Rudd became Prime Minister twice and gave the job straight over to Tony Abbott so who even knows anymore?

'*Prime Ministerial Powers*' include:

(a) the right to choose which Third World island nation can be used to indefinitely detain asylum seekers

(b) getting to meet Barack Obama, but then acting really cool about it afterwards, like it's no big deal

(c) first right of refusal in choosing which minority group to victimise to increase support in Western Sydney during a tight re-election campaign

(d) the right to gently rest your head on your Chief of Staff's shoulder while she feeds you spaghetti

(e) the right to call impromptu public holidays in the immediate aftermath of sporting victories (*arch.*)

(f) the right to simultaneously, and with a straight face, encourage citizens to take on more debt to finance investment properties, while insisting that a country should never be in deficit.

'*Campaign Trail*' means Western Sydney, and sometimes South Australia, if there's a good shipbuilding contract on offer.

# Australia's Electoral Contract

**1.0 Bill Shorten & Scott Morrison**

1.1 Subject to this provision, Bill Shorten and Scott Morrison agree to exercise the office of Prime Minister with dignity and restraint.

1.2 Clause 1.1 notwithstanding, Bill Shorten may at his discretion deliver as many as five (5) of the following, per working week:

(a) zingers;

(b) zing-a-lings;

(c) KFC Zinger Combos; or

(d) any other zinger-related wordplay.

1.3 Clause 1.1 notwithstanding, Scott Morrison may brush aside reasonable questions from Leigh Sales, with the phrase 'Fair dinkum', up to eight (8) times per *7:30* appearance.

1.4 Bill Shorten and Scott Morrison agree that they will ensure that their respective parties will not knife them within seven (7) days of taking office.

1.5 Bill Shorten agrees not to invite Kevin Rudd back to Kirribilli under any circumstances.

1.6 Scott Morrison agrees not to invite Joe Hockey back to Kirribilli under any circumstances (unless all the marble coffee tables have been packed away).

**2.0 Australian Voters**

2.1 Subject to this provision;

2.2 The Australian Voters agree to limit their election issues to a maximum of three (3) for the entire Campaign Trail.

2.3 The Australian Voters agree, notwithstanding their power in a democratic system, that the only accepted forms of political commentary and participation shall be:

(a) trying to get your tweet on-screen during *Q&A*

(b) getting into a fight at Christmas with their uncle who thinks that Cory Bernardi has 'got it right'; or

(c) posting *Simpsons* memes.

2.4 The Australian Voters agree to draw a maximum of ten (10) penises per ballot paper.

2.5 The Australian Voters agree to loudly defend their right to vote below the line, but then never actually vote below the line because oh my god this is taking forever I just want my sausage sizzle.

**3.0 Breach of Agreement**

3.1 If either Scott Morrison or Bill Shorten breach this Agreement, the Australian Voters have the power to;

(a) Elect them anyway; or

(b) *[subsection (b) deleted – please see s.5 and s.12 of the Hasty Amendment Regulations (Cth) 2016.]*

3.2 In the event that the Australian Voters breach this agreement by electing The Greens, they accept full responsibility for all television networks being nationalised to broadcast Scott Ludlam-programmed episodes of *Rage* on continuous loop.

3.3 In the event that the Australian Voters breach this agreement by electing a member of any Nick Xenophon aligned party, they accept that they may be subjected to endless publicity stunts involving hand-drawn placards, workers dressed in high-vis clothing and other props such as pillows, mattresses, novelty over-sized cheques and anything else that won't obscure Nick Xenophon's face from the camera.

# Australia's Electoral Contract

**SIGNED BY THE PARTIES**

| | | |
|---|---|---|
| *signature* | *signature* | *signature* [Voter: please sign here] |
| Bill Shorten | Scott Morrison | Who cares? |
| *name* | *name* | *name* |

**IN THE PRESENCE OF**

| | | |
|---|---|---|
| *signature* | *signature* | *signature* [Witness: please sign here] |
| Tanya Plibersek | Christopher Pyne | |
| *name* | *name* | *name* |
| Definitely Not A Faceless Man | BFF 4 lyfe | |
| *occupation* | *occupation* | *occupation* |

60 Seconds With...

# Penny Wong MP

**Penny Wong: How did The Shovel and The Chaser come to work together?**
The Shovel: Sorry, I thought we were asking the questions!

**PW: I'd think very carefully before continuing down that path.**
TS: Hang on, this is not how ...

**PW: It's an odd arrangement isn't it. Two satirical news organisations suddenly working together. How is this in Australia's national interest?**
TS: Wait, let's just start again.

**PW: Would you like to be pompous for the whole day, or just for this question?**
TS: I'm sorry Senator it's just that ...

**PW: I will remind you that you are under oath.**
TS: OK! OK! We're a satirical cartel in breach of the anti-collusion act!

**PW: Thank you. No further questions.**

Image: Labour Party

FORGOTTEN HISTORY

# The Real Story Behind The Tampa Crisis

By Captn. Charles Firth

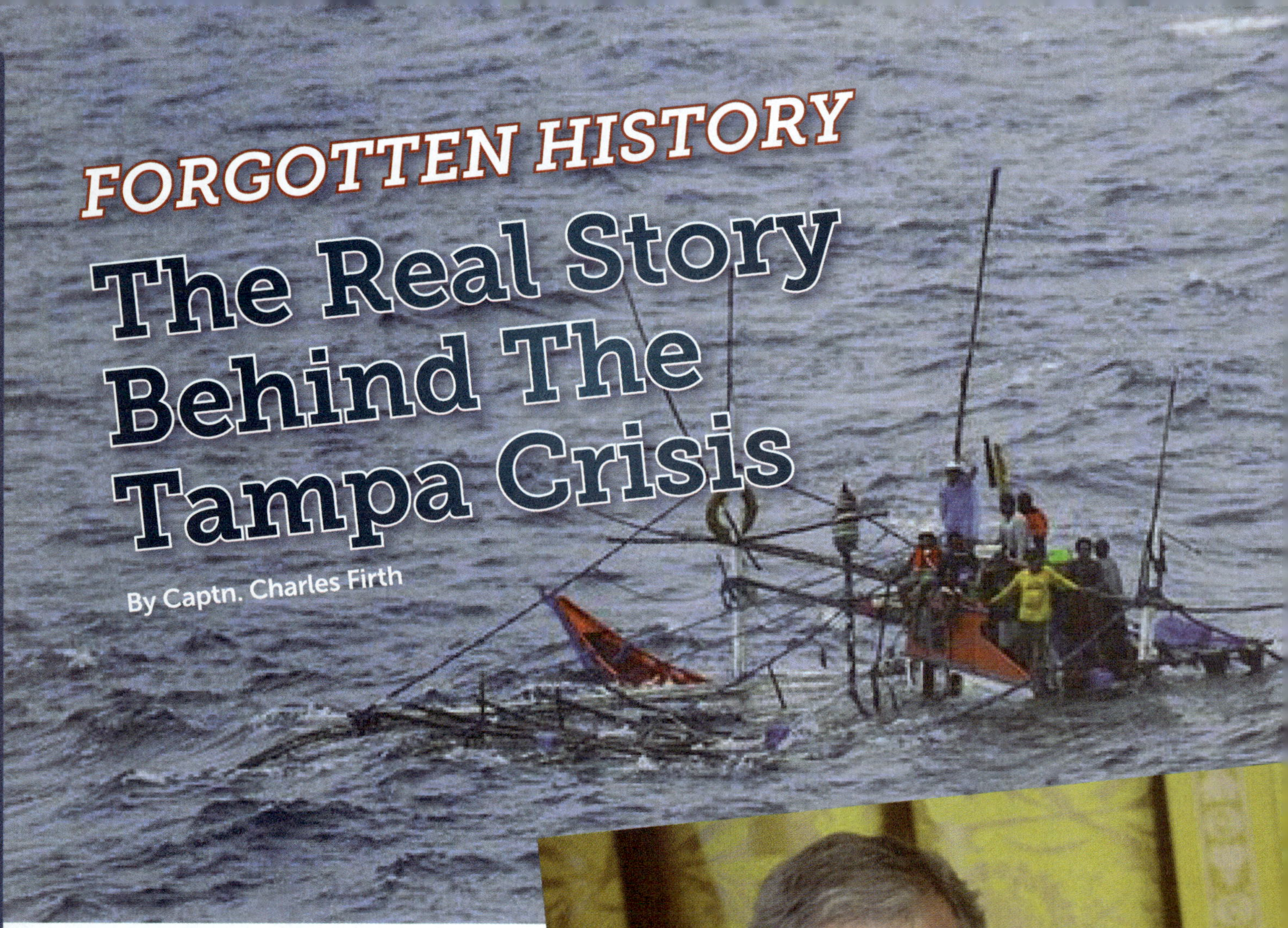

In January, 2001, Liberal Party strategists faced a seemingly insurmountable problem. Internal polling showed that John Howard was seen as "mean and tricky". Worse still, the Opposition leader Kim Beazley was consistently ahead in the polls.

"If you asked an average voter what the top three issues were at the beginning of 2001, they would have told you health, education and faster internet speeds for porn," recalls Shane Stone, the then Liberal Party President, "and Labor was ahead on all of those issues. The only way we could win was to shift the agenda onto our strengths. Like shitting on immigrants, or selling off public assets to our mates."

As the Parliament went into summer break, the Liberal Party was facing annihilation. Then, on Australia Day 2001, Howard's Chief of Staff, Arthur Sinodinos, had an idea.

"I was on my way to Kirribilli House, and I looked around at all the crowds, and it occurred to me that there was a lot of, shall we say, 'non-white' folks celebrating," recalls Sinodinos. "If we could tap into the votes of immigrants, then we might be able split them away from voting Labor, and get across the line."

He doubted Howard would go for it. Howard had said some unfortunate things about Asian immigration in the mid-1980s. But by this stage they were desperate, and anything was worth a try.

When Sinodinos arrived at Kirribilli House, he went straight up to John Howard and pitched the idea. If the Liberal Party could focus the attention of the electorate on the increasing ethnic diversity of Australia, then perhaps the Government was in with a chance.

Sinodinos himself was a first-generation Australian to Greek immigrant parents, he explained to Howard. He saw Australia's vibrant immigrant community as a key driver of Australia's prosperity.

"I love it," said John Howard to Sinodinos' surprise.

Howard explained that he still hated foreigners. He'd never understood why Australia couldn't just be a bunch of people who looked exactly like him. But he liked the view from Kirribilli House even more than his hatred of brown people. He was prepared to try anything. Even if it involved pretending to like immigrants.

"It will define my leadership. My legacy will be the gun buyback, and enduring tolerance towards brown people." In celebration, Howard raised a toast "to the browns, blacks, yellows and darkies."

The next day, Howard convened a cabinet meeting. Immigration Minister Philip Ruddock was immediately on board. Ruddock had been a lifelong member of Amnesty International mainly because he liked the badge, and yearned for a day when he could pretend he gave a shit about people fleeing for their lives.

Throughout the following months, he and most of the Federal cabinet started laying the groundwork for an election based on immigration. Whenever anything happened, Howard instructed his ministers to link that issue to immigration. Hospital waiting lists are too long? Make sure that people know that highly skilled immigrant doctors and nurses are the only thing preventing it from being longer. Schools underfunded? More immigration provides the economic growth required to see ongoing investment in education. Transport too congested? Many of the entry-level jobs are filled by non-skilled immigrants who work under conditions that Australian workers eschew.

Suddenly the sleeper issue of immigration, which had long been dormant, started to rise in the polls. By March it had cracked the top five issues. By May it was in the top three. By August, it was the top issue.

Though Labor Party strategists could see it happening, they were helpless in stopping it.

"We knew it in February," said one Labor insider. "But we had no idea what to do."

"You see, Kim Beazley had only become leader because his dad was a politician, and didn't really understand strategy."

Desperate, the Opposition hit upon a plan. They would all call their dads, who were all ex-politicians, and ask them for advice.

There was only one senior Labor MP who wasn't there because his dad was a politician: Mark Latham. "At that stage Mark Latham had pretty moderate views on immigration. He merely believed in the immediate execution of all immigrants," recalls the insider. "Obviously he became a lot more extreme later on."

Eventually they came up with a plan: the Labor Party would run on exactly the same policy as the Liberal Party, but with a different colour on the How to Vote cards. Now they just had to wait to find out what the Liberal Party policy on immigration would be.

Then, in August 2001, a Norwegian freighter rescued 433 refugees and then entered Australian waters. It sparked a crisis nobody had seen coming.

Sinodinos was elated. "These people fleeing Afghanistan were exactly the sort of people we wanted to encourage to come to Australia. People bravely fleeing murderous extremists and seeking a secure life in a stable democracy like Australia. This was a slam dunk for the Liberal Party. We could boast that Australia was leading the charge against Islamic extremism by giving safe harbour to the enemies of the Taliban."

"The MV Tampa was a perfect symbol of everything we'd been working towards all year," says Reith. "A boatload of refugees that Australia could welcome with open arms. Sure, we all hated reffos, but anything to win the election."

"I remember Peter Reith and Philip Ruddock bursting into the PM's office," recalls Sinodinos. "There was glee on all their faces. Ruddock exploded, 'We're going to win the election. If we just make a big deal about showing compassion and tolerance, the election is in the bag.'"

But something was wrong. John Howard's face had become pale. He look ill. "It was like he'd seen a ghost or something," recalls Reith.

It was at that point that John Howard revealed something to this small coterie of insiders, something which has remained secret until now. "We can't do it," said Howard, shaking slightly. He paused, then continued. "The thing is, I have submechanophobia."

The group stared blankly at Howard. None of them knew what Howard was talking about.

"Submechanophobia," Howard stammered, "is the fear of partially or fully submerged man-made objects. When I was young, I got mauled by a boat-shaped dog. Ever since, I've been afraid of boats.

If this strategy means that boats have to arrive in Australia, then I'm sorry, we can't do it."

The men in the room fell silent.

Ruddock pushed Howard on it. "What about planes? Are you scared of planes?"

"No no," Howard replied. "They're completely fine. It's just boats I'm scared of."

"Well you might have mentioned it a bit earlier," said Reith, furious. "We've just spent half a year priming the electorate to welcome immigrants, and now you turn around and say we can't welcome them with open arms because you're scared of the method of transport they're arriving on?!"

John Howard's wax model at Madame Tussauds was the first ever to be considered more lifelike than the model

At this point, Sinodinos intervened. He told John Howard, who was still trembling, to go home and lie down. He promised Howard they would find a way to spin it.

For the next six hours, Reith, Ruddock and Sinodinos sat around trying to work out how to get the Liberal Party out of this mess.

A few hours in, Tony Abbott poked his head around the corner. "The parliamentary kitchen is all out of raw onions," he said. "I don't suppose anyone has a spare raw onion?"

Stumped, the group invited Abbott to the brainstorm. They explained their predicament to Abbott.

"He immediately grasped the opportunity in front of us," said Ruddock. "What he said was pure genius. Or maybe I was just dazed from his onion-breath."

"We'll just have to go after racist voters," declared Abbott. "We'll imply that every problem with our hospitals, schools and roads is because of immigrants," declared Abbott. "But instead of openly saying it, we'll just say it's about stopping the boats. We'll imply we're concerned for the safety of the people on the boats or something."

It hadn't even occurred to anyone in the room that an openly racist policy was possible or even desirable. Would there be enough racist voters in Australia, Sinodinos pondered?

The group burst into laughter. Of course there would be. And the great thing was, many of them would be Labor voters.

But there were two ministers who were appalled. Philip Ruddock, a long-time member of Amnesty International, didn't want to lose his badge. Same for Peter Reith, who was quitting politics that election to pursue his true passion: amateur photography.

Both Ruddock and Reith left that meeting determined to upend Abbott's plan, whatever the cost.

Within weeks, Ruddock had an idea that he believed would derail the "stop the boats" campaign forever. On September 28, 2001, Philip Ruddock announced to parliament the "Pacific Solution".

It was a heavy handed policy which prevented asylum seekers receiving legal access. It was a clear breach of international law, and violated human rights.

By blatantly contravening international law, Ruddock thought, Australia would be immediately condemned by the rest of the world, and the plan would have to be abandoned. Australia could go back to having an Open Borders policy.

Instead, to Ruddock's dismay, the Pacific Solution was lauded around the world as a sensible solution to the problem of poor refugees. The Labor Party, as per Beazley's plan, announced that they supported Ruddock's approach, but would change the colour on all the policy documents to red.

It was up to Reith to stop a policy that had only come into existence thanks to John Howard's fear of boats. In a last ditch effort, the Defence Minister decided to release a batch of photos the Navy had taken which showed a refugee boat sinking.

The images were powerful. It showed children floating in the sea, their boat half-sunk, with their parents heroically rescuing them. Reith knew that if these images came out, compassion for the poor innocent children and their desperate parents would skyrocket. Perhaps that would derail Abbott's ridiculous plan. However, Reith, an avid amateur photographer had just done a course on cropping photographs, and decided that the composition of the images would be more powerful if he applied some of the principles he'd learnt in the course.

The next day Reith read the newspapers with dismay. He had inadvertently cropped out the sinking boat, so it looked like the children in the sea had been thrown there by their parents, rather than being there because their boat was already sinking. Sure, the images really popped, but they were misleading. And nothing he said could convince the press that the refugee parents were the innocent victims of a cropping mistake.

Most fears have a social aspect. When a leader fears something, no matter how irrationally, those fears tend to spread. By the time of the election, Australia was faced with widespread submechanophobia.

Unfortunately, one of the most suggestible Australians was the Opposition Leader himself. "Kim Beazley was very suggestible," recalls one party insider. "If you suggested to him that he should have another sausage roll, bam, he'd have one. Same with submechanophobia. The moment it was suggested he should fear boats, he immediately started getting really scared of them. As soon as that happened, I knew we'd lost the election."

It's a fear that remains almost 20 years later. Polls suggest that 85% of Australians suffer from severe submechanophobia.

"The problem facing Australia is that the best way to get rid of an irrational fear is through exposure therapy," said one Labor strategist. "But you can't expose voters to boats when they never arrive. It's like they're afraid of ghosts -- they don't even exist."

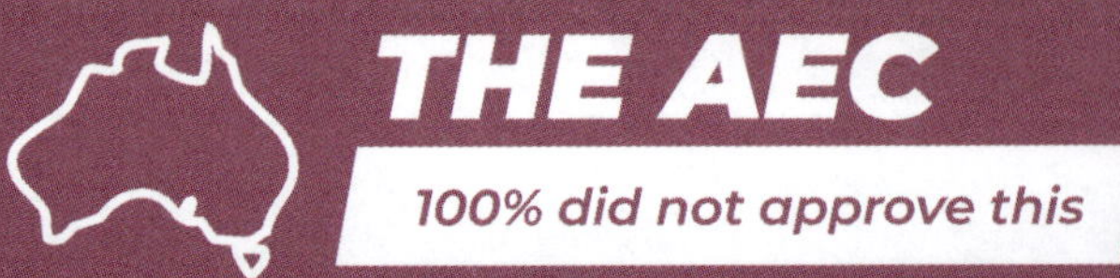


# The Official™ Guide

## To voting in the 2019 election

**When you come to vote on election day, you'll be given two ballot papers – one the size of the snacks menu at a bar, the other the size of a king size bed sheet. So what's the difference between the two, and how is your vote counted?**

### VOTING IN THE HOUSE OF REPRESENTATIVES

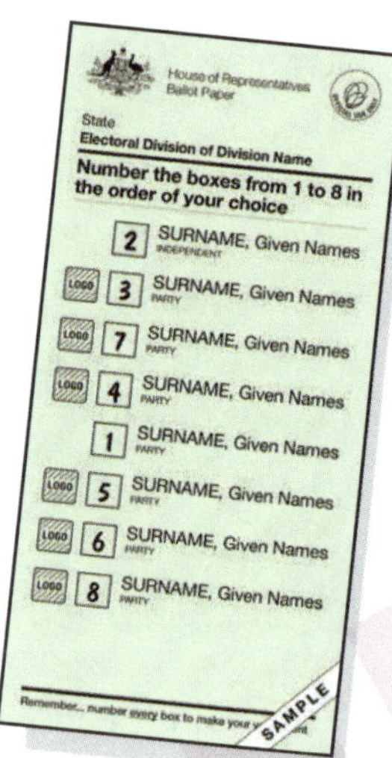


This is the smaller of the two ballot papers, and usually contains around 6 or 7 candidates – one from each of the major parties, one local resident who organised the primary school fete last year and naively thought they would be suited to politics, and one former Liberal female MP who was bullied out of the party and is now running as an independent.

You have the choice to either follow a party-endorsed how to vote card or take a risk and follow your own fucking intuition.

If you choose not to use a how-to-vote card, remember to put a number in each box, giving each candidate a score out of 10. Simple.

When you're finished, simply put your ballot paper in the box, or if you're a Greens voter, in the recycling bin.

### VOTING IN THE SENATE

Australia's Senate system is a straightforward, democratic process whereby you simply put a 1 in the box next to your preferred major party candidate, in order to elect a former taxi-driver from Narre Warren who is now the leader of the 'Equal Rights for Rose-Breasted Cockatoos Party'.

You do have the option to fill in every box below the line, an arduous task which requires you to make a range of split-second judgments such as 'Is the Reclaim Australia Party more weird and racist than the Love Australia Or Leave Party?' and 'Do I care more about animals or old people?'

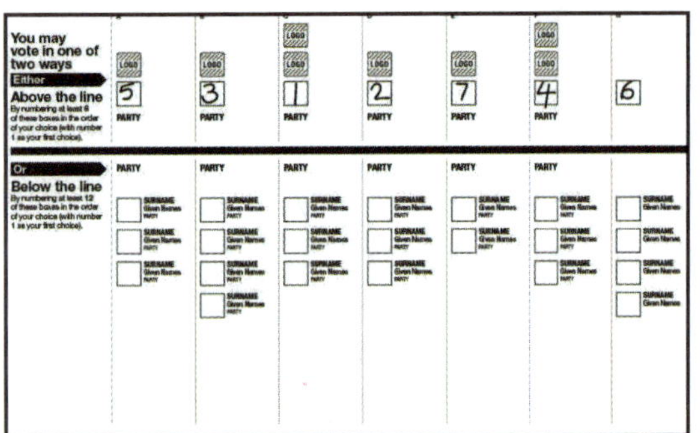


Once you have finished filling in your Senate ballot paper, simply fold it in half, fold it in half again, then fold it in half again, before placing it in the ballot box, realising it won't fit, folding it in half again, and then just scrunching the fucking thing into a ball and stuffing it in halfway.

Once voting closes, ballot papers are handed to Australian Electoral Commission staff who study the array of boxes and numbers carefully before putting the papers away in a cupboard and drawing the successful candidates' names from a hat.

# The Official™
## Demonstration Ballot Paper

**Want to practice throwing away your vote before polling day? No problem we've included a test ballot below for you to invalidate.**

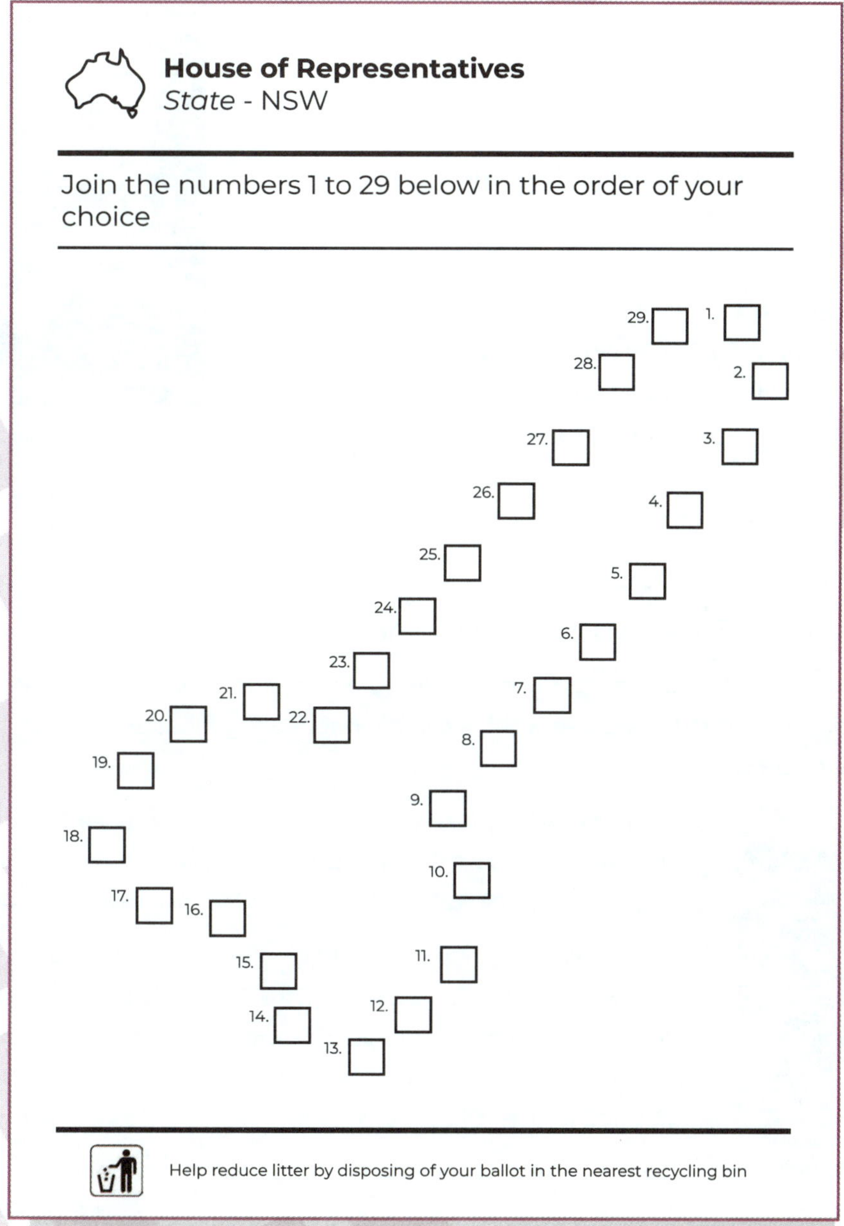


**Note:** Always be sure to draw the entire cock and balls by hand. Many voters make the mistake of trying to save time by simply ticking the box next to the first cock they see, and end up voting for Cory Bernardi.

# Bill Shorten

*This article refers to the Australian Labor leader Bill Shorten. For the real leader of the Australian Opposition, see Tony Jones (ABC personality).*

The Honourable
**Bill Shorten MP**
(At least until ICAC is done with him)

Image: Ross Caldwell / Flickr

**Bill Shorten** (focus group approved 12 May, 1967) is an Australian politician and the first Opposition Leader in history to fail to oppose anything.

### Early Life

Bill Shorten was made in a mid-sized electronics parts warehouse in Melbourne's inner west.

Shorten later said that growing up as a robot in Melbourne in the 1970s was challenging, but on the plus side his family lived on the smell of an oily rag.

After software upgrades at St Mary's Catholic Primary School, Xavier College and Monash University, Bill briefly worked as a sleep consultant at Royal Melbourne Hospital. He would talk to patients about his plans for building a stronger Australia, instantly curing their insomnia.

### Union career

In 1994 Bill began his career in the union movement, a unique pathway that allows aspiring Labor politicians to mix with a truly diverse range of other aspiring Labor politicians.

Years later in his maiden speech to parliament, Shorten said it was his time in union management that gave him a genuine insight into what ordinary Aussies want in life. "A roof over their heads, food on the table, and a safe Labor seat in federal parliament".

Shorten, moments before challenging Morrison to settle the election in the local Maccas carpark.

He promised to make it his mission to deliver those basic needs for all Australians. Except the safe Labor seats, which he wanted to make very clear had already been assigned for the next three decades.

Shorten first came to national attention during the Beaconsfield mining disaster of 2006. Some critics at the time said Shorten was there purely to increase his media profile. But without any experience in mining, mine rescues or disaster management, he was actually uniquely qualified for the role.

When the mine disaster was finally resolved, Shorten chose to move to another massive hole, Canberra.

**Political life**

In 2005 Shorten announced that he would seek pre-selection for the federal seat of Maribyrnong, even though it was already held by sitting member Bob Sercombe. He justified the challenge, saying, "We haven't won a federal election since 1993. When your footy team loses four consecutive grand finals, you renew the team". The new sporting metaphor plugin he'd had installed the week before had just paid for itself.

Shorten, learning he's about to become PM just as the housing market has crashed.

Once in parliament, Shorten played a pivotal role in the overthrow of Kevin Rudd, claiming that Labor desperately needed the fresh approach of Julia Gillard to lead them into the future. He later played a pivotal role in the overthrow of Julia Gillard, saying that Labor desperately needed the fresh approach of Kevin Rudd to lead them into the future.

As leader himself now, Shorten says he occasionally has an urge to knife himself, purely out of habit. "Once in a while I'll hit the phones to start doing the numbers against me. It's a habit I've got to kick," he confided. Bill Shorten says he has his full support.

**Opposition Leader**

Shorten has been desperately unpopular for most of his time as Opposition Leader, with many seeing him as aloof, unconvincing or awkward.

To address the issue, Bill took a conversation night class at CAE in 2014, on the recommendation of his advisors. The results paid immediate dividends when, during a media event at Queanbeyan Woolies, Mr Shorten asked a shopper, "What's your favourite type of lettuce?" before seamlessly pivoting to his killer follow up, "Do you eat a lot of salad?"

The exchange proved that Shorten not only had the people skills to sway a swinging voter, he could provide valuable grocery data insights too.

Pictured: Artist's impression of Bill's twin brother Robert

**Personal life**

Bill has a twin brother, Robert, who often fills in for him during question time or during media interviews. If elected, Bill will run the country, Monday-Wednesday with Robert taking over the reins Thursdays and Fridays.

**Dear Pollypedia readers:**
We are a small non-profit (in the very literal sense) that runs the 500,000,000th top website in the world. We have only 500 staff, but serve content up to almost 4 people daily, some of them not relatives. If everyone who used our site gave just $5, this fundraiser could be over in an hour, and we'd also be able to afford coffee for about three days. So please, give generously, and we promise we won't bug you again for at least three weeks.

**No, fuck off. X**

# Scott Morrison

*This article refers to the Prime Minister of Australia Scott Morrison. For the actual current ruler of Australia, see Rupert Murdoch (billionaire raisin).*

Scott John Morrison (born 13 May 1968) is an Australian politician serving as the 3057th and current[citation needed] Prime Minister of Australia. As the leader of the governing Liberal Party, Morrison is responsible for making decisions about the future of Australia, and then double checking with the right wing of his party if it is the correct decision.

The Honourable

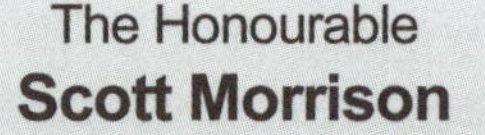


Prime Minister (Last checked 3/3/2019)

**Born:** 1968
**Died:** 2019
**Cause of death:** Beheaded by comedian Becky Lucas

Image: Commonwealth of Australia 2016

## Early life

Scott Morrison was created during a brainstorming session at a Sydney advertising agency in the late 1990s.

Initially the plan was to create a prototype for the quintessential 'fair-dinkum Aussie Dad'. But after a few beers, the ad creatives thought it would be more fun to make him a dickhead. No-one knows where the weird Christian bit came from.

## Early career

After spending thirty years as a regional salesman at a small photocopy distributor, Morrison became head of Tourism Australia. He oversaw the 'Where The Bloody Hell Are You?' campaign, widely regarded as one of the least successful in the organisation's history.

The campaign showed that Morrison lacked judgment, possessed questionable money-management skills and had a tendency to misread the mood of the nation. The Liberal Party snapped him up immediately.

Scott Morrison was inspired to create the 'Where the bloody hell are you?' campaign after witnessing Michaelia Cash disappear behind a whiteboard.

### Political career

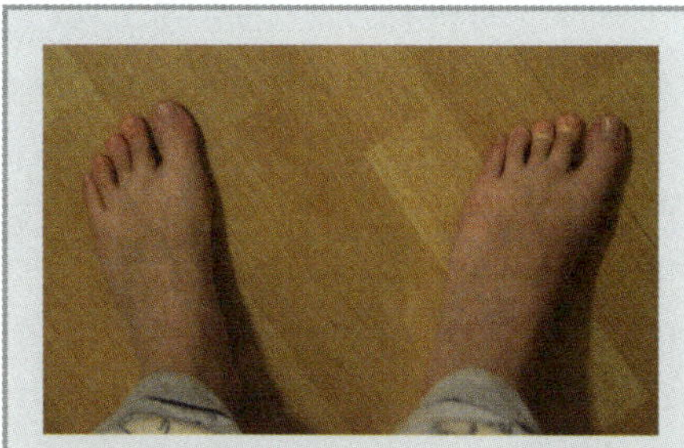

Pictured: Scott Morrison's feet, according to his staff.

Morrison entered parliament in 2007 and was moved to the shadow front bench a year later. But it was in 2012, when Tony Abbott chose Morrison to implement his 'stop the boats' policy, that the member for Cook's political career really took off. Having so successfully stopped people coming to Australia during his time as head of Tourism Australia, Morrison was considered the perfect man for the job.

In what was to become one of the most effective campaigns todissuade asylum seekers, Morrison organised the 'Where The Bloody Hell Are You?' campaign to be shown in the Middle East, Africa and South East Asia. The flow of people to Australia immediately dried up.

After the success of the program, a friend gave Morrison a small model boat featuring the words 'I stopped these'. The boat sits next to Morrison's model of a small tourist featuring the words 'I stopped these'.

After 13 months as Immigration Minister, Morrison moved to a new role as Social Services Minister. Morrison said that after months working with asylum seekers, it was nice to be working with humans again.

In one of his first speeches as Social Services Minister Morrison said he wanted to search the sewage of welfare recipients to see if he could find traces of drugs. Close friends at the time said it was the clearest sign yet that Morrison's drug addiction was spiralling out of control.

In 2017 Morrison famously brought what appeared to be a piece of coal into question time, passing it around to fascinated colleagues. It was later confirmed to be Rupert Murdoch.

In August 2018 Morrison defeated Peter Dutton in a leadership spill to become Prime Minister. Wanting to bring a bit of gravitas to the role, Morrison immediately started wearing board shorts and surfing caps.

### Personal life

Pictured: Scott Morrison at home with his significant other.

Scott Morrison is a member of the Assemblies of God Church. Services are known to include 'speaking in tongues', where a simple English phrase like 'Love thy neighbour as thyself' can be translated as 'use thy neighbour's place as a prison to lock up small children'.

Morrison lives in Sydney with his wife, his two daughters and a pair of two left shoes.

# Pauline Hanson

*This article refers to the Australian politician and former prison inmate Pauline Hanson. For the 90s boyband 'Hanson' see 1990s crimes against humanity.*

Senator
**Pauline Hanson**
Racist.

Image: Rick Dikeman / Wikipedia

**Pauline Hanson** is a bigot with links to far-right racist groups, and a part time Sunrise guest presenter. Known for her outspoken views against ethnic people, Mrs Hanson was expelled as a sitting member of the Liberal Party in 1992 for her outspoken views, which were derided by Prime Minister John Howard as 'stealing some of my best talking points'.

Best known for her catch-phrase "Yes, I certainly am xenophobic", Hanson has spent the last 30 years of her career in a tireless crusade to convince the general public about the superiority of the white race, a position largely undermined every time Hanson opens her mouth.

### Early Life

Pauline Hanson was born in Kenya in 1962.

### Fish and Chip shop

Before entering politics Hanson ran a small fish and chip shop, where her preference for white flesh was considered far less controversial.

### Political life

Hanson rose to prominence in politics after a string of interviews by the media successfully decimated her platform, and certainly didn't just give her racism a platform into people's homes. As a result, Hanson was never heard of again after the 1996 federal election, except for the hours of media coverage dedicated to destroying her platform when she ran for office again in 1998, 2001, 2004, 2009, 2010, 2011, 2013, 2015 and 2019.

Pictured: Hanson expresses her views against mixing colours with whites after her favourite uniform was stained bright red in the wash.

Image: Flickr / arete13

In 2010, Hanson announced her intention to move to the United Kingdom, however this plan was cancelled shortly after, with Hanson expressing shock at how un-welcoming the UK is to immigrants.

In 2018, Hanson protested the wearing of burqas by becoming the first and only person to wear a burqua in parliament - a move that was described as a "great improvement" by fellow senators, who then unanimously voted to make the obscuring of Hanson's face permanent.

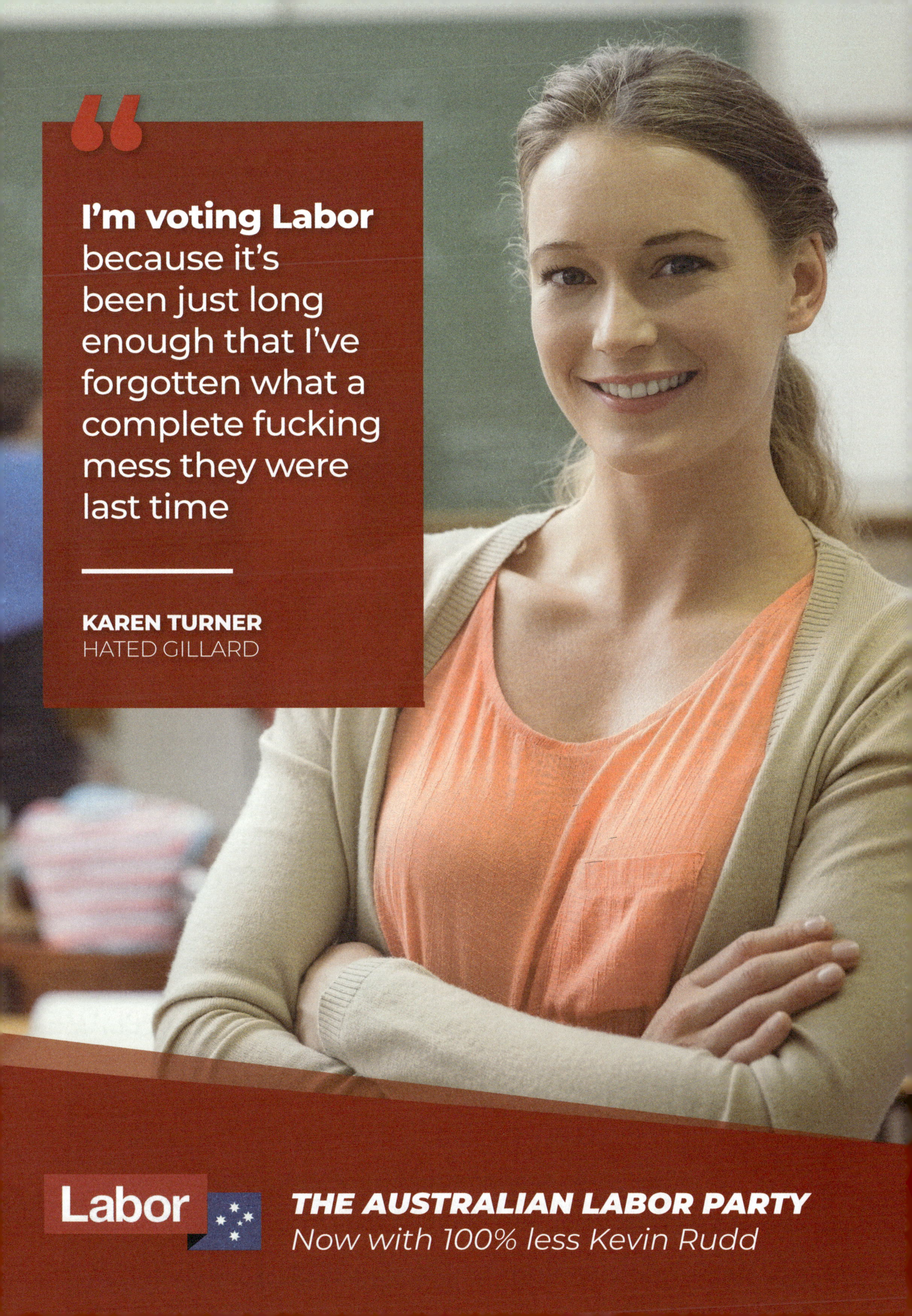

“

**I’m voting Labor** because it’s been just long enough that I’ve forgotten what a complete fucking mess they were last time

**KAREN TURNER**
HATED GILLARD

***THE AUSTRALIAN LABOR PARTY***
*Now with 100% less Kevin Rudd*

ADVERTISEMENT

# IMPORTANT PUBLIC MEETING

PAULINE HANSON INVITES YOU TO A SPECIAL INVESTIGATION INTO HOW THE AUSTRALIA POST GUY GETS THE LETTERS OUT OF THE POST BOX, GIVEN THEY'RE ALL THE WAY DOWN THE BOTTOM AND YOU CAN'T FIT YOUR HAND THROUGH THE SLOT.

"IT SCARES ME, AND IT SHOULD SCARE YOU TOO"

WED 19TH JUNE - GATTON SHIRE HALL - 7PM

## SPEAKERS:

MALCOLM ROBERTS
ARE POSTIES ACTUALLY ALIENS?

MARK LATHAM
HOW I BROKE MY ARM TRYING TO GET THE LETTERS OUT OF THE BOX.

PAULINE HANSON
WHY MUSLIMS ARE TO BLAME.

VOTE ONE 1 NATION

FOR MORE INFO CONTACT MALCOLM ROBERTS TELEPATHICALLY
OR VISIT OUR FACEBOOK AT HTTPS://WWW.FACEBOOK.COM/PAGE/ON

# Richard Di Natale

*This article refers to the Australian Greens leader Richard Di Natale. For the creepy Steve Jobs looking guy from that mattress ad, see Richard De Rucci.*

**Scott Ludlam** (born in New Zealand and never bothered to check his citizenship like an idiot) is surprisingly not the leader of the Australian Greens.

Instead that title goes to the much more forgettable Richard Di Natale, and that's about as much information as we have on that guy.

The Honourable

**MP Ricky D.**

Couldn't afford an Uber

Image: Victorian Greens / Flickr

### Early Life

We assume Richard was born at some point though frankly we don't care enough to look it up. I think we can safely assume he had a childhood and went to school. He's in the Greens so he probably wasted enough years at university to get a doctorate in some baloney like 'Weed smoking' or 'Carbon induced climate change and its destabilising effects on the viability of the insect biomass over the next 100 years'.

### Political career

Presumably Richard was elected to either the Senate or House of Representatives at some point, and basically just had to sit around and wait long enough for the three other Greens MPs to retire in order to take on the top job.

Richard Di Natale casually leans on Australia's largest solar far, blissfully unaware his shadow has just knocked out power from one tenth of South Australian homes.

Image: Jeremy Buckingham / Flickr

### Private life

Di Natale is a keen member of the 'rolling coal' movement, and spends most of his downtime needlessly driving his diesel 4WD around his neighbourhood.

When not on the road Richard can be found turning all the lights on around his house, burning large piles of garbage in his palatial fireplace, and pouring bottles of kerosene into his local lake.

Richard has described himself as 'not a politician at heart' and has promised his wife that he will only run for Parliament 20-30 more times before giving up and pursuing his dream of sitting on the board of a bank.

# Clive Palmer

*This article refers to the failed Australian politician and former billionaire. For the Australian national treasure, see Chive Palmie (chicken based pub meal).*

**Clive Palmer** (incorporated 26 March, 1954) is a billionaire mining magnate and dinosaur theme park owner, who ran for parliament on a platform of being more in touch with the common man than the average politician, which sadly is probably true.

Having made his fortune flipping houses at a young age, Palmer has since used his immense wealth to give back to humanity, with projects like building a giant ship called the Titanic, opening a giant dinosaur theme-park, and various other ideas he stole from popular 90s blockbusters.

In 2017 Palmer was taken to court for the crime of destroying jobs after shutting down a profitable nickel mine, and the much more serious crime of publishing a book of poetry.

A widely loved national treasure, in 2012 Palmer decided to put an end to this by going into politics, before leaving politics entirely in 2017 after declaring he had solved all the problems and there was nothing more for him to do.

The Deplorable
**Clive Palmer AO**
The Diet Pepsi of Donald Trumps

Fans of Palmer have demonstrated their love of his comic nature by adding Charlie Chaplin moustaches to his posters.

Image: Perth Jaywalker \ Wikipedia

Clive Palmer, dressed as a rabbit, says he is sick and tired of people who treat politics like a joke.

### Early Life

Clive was born into difficult circumstances, with an unemployed mother and a father who only owned a small radio station, a measly tyre company, and a shabby, largely forgettable travel agency which could barely cover the cost of all the free round-the-world trips the family were forced to partake in just to escape the horrors of their middle class existence.

In 1973 Palmer went to university to study politics, before quitting halfway through the course when he got bored, an experience which he has described as inspiring his future political career.

After dropping out of university Palmer instead decided to turn his hand to real estate, making an impressive $40 million from a mere $50 million loan from his father.

The rest of his life is largely a mystery as Palmer unfortunately suffered complete memory loss as of May 2017, which also happened to coincide with the trial over his questionable liquidation of Queensland Nickel.

# John Howard, The Ghost of

*This article refers to the former Australian Prime Minister. For the Australian actor, simply replace the words 'Australian Parliament' with 'Sea Change' and it's basically right.*

The Honourable
**John Howard**
Threw kids off a boat

**The haunting spectre of John Howard** (retroactively dreamed into existence by rose-tinted Liberals c. 2012) is a former Australian politician whose middling success at not being a complete fuckup has haunted Australian Prime Ministers ever since he left office in 2007. Though many have attempted to imitate his amazing talent of selling off public assets to fund tax breaks for boomers during one of the country's most prosperous boom periods, none so far have matched his legacy of short-sighted voter-pleasing policies at the expense of the long-term prosperity.

Howard is best remembered today as the man who promised to solve the issue of asylum seekers if re-instated in the 2004 election, a pledge he says he plans on following through on any day now.

### Early Life

John Winston Howard was born on the 26th July 1839 after two large fluffy caterpillars crawled across a lump of canned ham. Howard is described by family and friends as having been a regular child, who enjoyed all the usual pastimes, from railing against business taxes to selling the toys he had enjoyed playing with to ensure his younger brother would never live to see such benefits. In 1948, Howard saw Donald Bradman play cricket at the SCG, and experienced his first orgasm (pictured right).

Howard attended Sydney University in 1958 where he became leader of the Liberal Club, a small student organisation that championed the ideals of smaller government, liberal economics, and selling out those first two beliefs if anyone with a chequebook comes along.

Pictured: John Howard learns who the current Liberal Party leader is

Image: Robert Keating/DFAT

### Political career

In 1974 Howard decided to run for political office, reasoning there just weren't enough ex-Sydney University lawyers in parliament. After winning his seat, in 1975 Howard was appointed Minister for Business in the new Frasier government, before being promoted to Treasurer in 1977.

Given that his time as treasurer oversaw the greatest recession the country has seen since the 1930s, he was fired and was never heard of again.

# 2019 ELECTORATE GUIDE

All 150 electorates, and why yours is the worst

# NEW SOUTH WALES

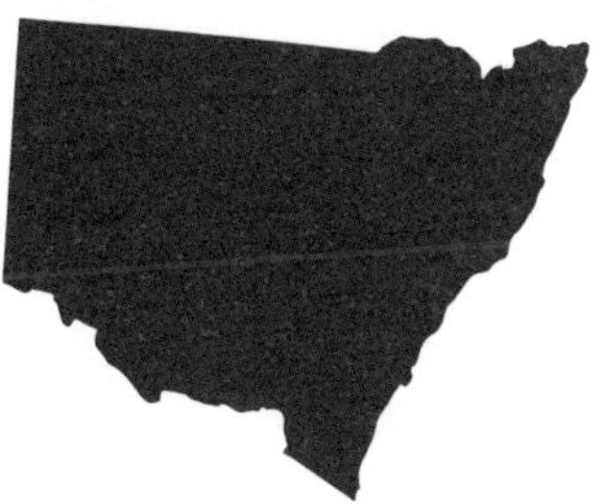

## Banks N.S.W.

Sitting Member: **David Coleman (Liberal)**

Margin: 1.44%

Profile: As the member for Banks, David Coleman fights hard to represent the interests of ANZ, CBA, NAB and Westpac. Much like every other member of the Liberal Party.

## Barton N.S.W.

Sitting Member: **Linda Burney (Labor)**

Margin: 8.3%

Profile: Named after Australia's first Prime Minister who is widely known for his work in creating the trivia question 'Who was Australia's first Prime Minister?'

## Bennelong N.S.W.

Sitting Member: **John Alexander (Liberal)**

Margin: 9.72%

Profile: The people of Bennelong voted in John Howard for 33 consecutive years. Bennelong is the Aboriginal word for 'Stockholm Syndrome'.

## Berowra N.S.W.

Sitting Member: **Julian Lesser (Liberal)**

Margin: 16.45%

Profile: Former Berowra member Philip Ruddock will be remembered as the only Australian politician to occupy a seat in parliament for 16 years after his death.

## Blaxland N.S.W.

Sitting Member: **Jason Clare (Labor)**

Margin: 19.48%

Profile: The seat made famous by Paul Keating, who paved the way for working class aspirationals, by moving from a fibro house in Bankstown to a grand home in Woollahra, with a collection of French clocks, Armani suits and Paul Keating memorabilia.

## Bradfield N.S.W.

Sitting Member: **Paul Fletcher (Liberal)**

Margin: 21.04%

Profile: In 2008 Paul Fletcher wrote a book called *Wired Brown Land? Telstra's Battle for Broadband*, the highest selling book on Telstra's Battle for Broadband in Australia that year.

## Calare N.S.W.

Sitting Member: **Andrew Gee (Liberal)**

Margin: 11.81%

Profile: Andrew Gee rose to fame in the early 00s as host of singing competition Australian Idol. He made the switch to politics in 2011, but continues as a television host under the stage name Osher Günsberg.

## Did you know?

During Scott Morrison's time as Immigration Minister, the number of people who came to Australia was zero, which coincidentally was also the number of people who came to Australia when Morrison was head of Tourism Australia.

## Chifley N.S.W.

Sitting Member: **Ed Husic (Labor)**

Margin: 19.9%

This seat is named after former Labor Prime Minister Ben Chifley, a heavy smoker who once walked all the way up to the top of a hill, just to get a light. It later made for a great speech. Before entering politics, Ed Husic worked in the union movement, one of only 190 of his Labor colleagues to have done so.

## Cook N.S.W.

Sitting Member: **Scott Morrison (Liberal)**

Margin: 15.39%

Scott Morrison was created during a brainstorming session at a Sydney advertising agency in the late 1990s. Initially the plan was to create a prototype for the quintessential 'fair-dinkum Aussie Dad'. But after a few beers, the ad creatives thought it would be more fun to make him a dickhead. No-one knows where the weird Christian bit came from.

## Cowper N.S.W.

Sitting Member: **Luke Hartsuyker (National)**

Margin: We're keeping it secret

Before entering politics Luke Hartsuyker owned and managed Clog Barn, Coffs Harbour's second biggest tourist attraction, and the only one to have a clog-shaped swimming pool. Not content that he was weird and eccentric enough, he joined the National Party.

## Cunningham N.S.W.

Sitting Member: **Sharon Bird (Labor)**

Margin: 13.32%

Sharon Bird was a high school teacher before entering politics. Since joining parliament she says she misses the maturity of her year 9 students.

## Dobell N.S.W.

Sitting Member: **Emma McBride (Labor)**

Margin: 4.81%

This seat was made famous by Craig Thompson who once used a union credit card to pay for a new suit and sex with prostitutes. Buying suits is of course against union protocol.

## Farrer N.S.W.

Sitting Member: **Sussan Ley (Liberal)**

Margin: 20.93%

As member for the NSW seat of Farrer, Sussan Ley has taken 27 tax-payer funded trips to the Gold Coast to ~~check on her property portfolio~~ undertake vital community work for her electorate in NSW.

## Fowler N.S.W.

Sitting Member: **Chris Hayes (Labor)**

Margin: 17.49%

As 'Chief Opposition Whip', Chris Hayes wants you all to know that the 'safe word' is 'applesauce'.

## Gilmore N.S.W.

Sitting Member: **Ann Sudmalis (Liberal) - retiring**

Margin: 0.73%

Warren Mundine is the new Liberal Party candidate for Glimore. He is a former ALP national president, once ran for the senate on a Labor ticket and doesn't live anywhere near the Gilmore electorate, but otherwise ticks all the boxes.

## Grayndler N.S.W.

Sitting Member: **Anthony Albanese (Labor)**

Margin: Not telling

Anthony Albanese will be best known as the guy who ruined Labor's re-election chances in 2022 when he foolishly attempted a leadership spill two weeks after Labor's return to office.

## Greenway N.S.W.

Sitting Member: **Michelle Rowland (Labor)**

Margin: 6.31%

Greenway is named after Francis Greenway, a convict who was transported to Australia after being found guilty of forgery. He later reformed and went on to write the best-selling novel Doliver Kwist.

# Eden-Monaro N.S.W.

Sitting member: **Mike Kelly (Labor)**

Left blank due to lack of media interest in this seat.

## THE ELECTORATES AUSTRALIA* FORGOT

### Fraser VIC.

Sitting Member: **New seat**

Notional margin: 20.6% to Labor

This newly created electorate is expected to start out right wing, then gradually become left wing over time.

### Watson N.S.W.

Sitting Member: **Tony Burke (Labor)**

Margin: 8.9%

Named after former Australian cricketer Shane Watson, expect the result of this seat to be reviewed by the third umpire.

### Whitlam N.S.W.

Sitting Member: **Stephen Jones (Labor)**

Margin: 6.9%

It would be tempting to dismiss this seat. And we have.

### Werriwa N.S.W.

Sitting Member: **Laurie Ferguson (Labor) - retiring**

Margin: 6.5%

The former seat of Mark Latham, the Labor Party would prefer to forget this seat ever existed. Which is why they parked Laurie Ferguson here for the past nine years. Thanks to a redistribution, it is now safely Labor, unless Shorten really, really stuffs up. So keep an eye on it.

### Bean A.C.T.

Sitting Member: **New seat**

Notional margin: 8.9% to Labor

Astoundingly, people are actually moving TO Canberra, which has led to the creation of a whole new seat. Yes. TO Canberra. We're having a bit of trouble process this information.

*Our print designer

## Hughes N.S.W.

Sitting Member: **Craig Kelly (Liberal)**

Margin: 9.33%

Profile: Craig Kelly was set to miss out on preselection, following a grassroots campaign to oust him. He was saved by Scott Morrison who said the party couldn't afford to lose another conservative middle-aged white male.

## Hume N.S.W.

Sitting Member: **Angus Taylor (Liberal)**

Margin: 10.18%

Profile: In 2003 Energy Minister Angus Taylor began a decades-long fight against wind. At the time of printing the wind was winning.

## Hunter N.S.W.

Sitting Member: **Joel Fitzgibbon (Labor)**

Margin: 12.46%

Profile: This seat used to be called Charlton, but was renamed Hunter after it shot and killed the original Hunter.

## Kingsford Smith N.S.W.

Sitting Member: **Matt Thistlethwaite (Labor)**

Margin: 8.57%

Profile: This seat, which is home to Sydney's airport, is held by former Transport Workers Union organiser Matt Thistlethwaite. If you don't vote for Matt, expect to be fisted at customs while your luggage makes its way to Fiji.

## Lindsay N.S.W.

Sitting Member: **Emma Husar (Labor - ret.)**

Margin: 1.11%

Profile: Whoever ends up with this seat will need to balance the interests of welfare bludgers and Western Sydney's nouveau riche. (Pro tip: If you have more than one Commodore up on bricks in the front yard, you're nouveau riche).

## Lyne N.S.W.

Sitting Member: **David Gillespie (National)**

Margin: 11.63%

Profile: David Gillespie was a gastroenterologist for 20 years. He decided to switch to politics, saying he wanted to work with even bigger arseholes.

## Macarthur N.S.W.

Sitting Member: **Michael Freelander (Labor)**

Margin: 8.33%

Profile: This seat has changed hands multiple times throughout its history, being designated a 'bellweather' seat by Antony Green (not to be confused with a bellend seat, which is the one where Tony Abbott is running)

## Mackellar N.S.W.

Sitting Member: **Jason Falinski (Liberal)**

Margin: 15.7%

Profile: Mackellar was held for years by Bronwyn Bishop before Jason Faliniski was helicoptered into this seat to replace her.

## Macquarie N.S.W.

Sitting Member: **Susan Templeman (Labor)**

Margin: 2.19%

Profile: This electorate got its name after a law was passed requiring one of everything in NSW to be named Macquarie.

## McMahon N.S.W.

Sitting Member: **Chris Bowen (Labor)**

Margin: 12.11%

Profile: This electorate is named after William McMahon who until recently was regarded as Australia's worst Prime Minister. He's now ranked sixth worst.

## Mitchell N.S.W.

Sitting Member: **Alex Hawke (Liberal)**

Margin: 17.82%

Profile: As a member of the Hillsong Church, Alex Hawke is the only MP who can say 'Fuck off we're full" in seven ancient languages. In one of his lighter monologues, Alan Jones dubbed Hawke 'A Cancer on the Liberal Party'.

## Newcastle N.S.W.

Sitting Member: **Sharon Claydon (Labor)**

Margin: 13.84%

Profile: The seat of Newcastle started out as a small town centred around a mine and the seat remains a massive hole to this day.

## New England N.S.W.

Sitting Member: **Barnaby Joyce (National)**

Margin: 0.09% (actually, that's Barnaby's average blood alcohol reading - *ed*)

Profile: Barnaby Joyce is a strong believer in the sanctity of marriage.

## North Sydney N.S.W.

Sitting Member: **Trent Zimmerman (Liberal)**

Margin: 13.61%

Profile: Former member for North Sydney Joe Hockey used to charge members $22,000 to be a part of his Free Enterprise Foundation. The going rate to hear Joe Hockey speak is now around $4.95.

## Page N.S.W.

Sitting Member: **Kevin Hogan (National)**

Margin: 2.3%

Profile: Do you believe that vaccinating your child causes AIDS? Are you of the opinion that sleeping with amethyst crystals in your anus can cure pancreatic cancer? Do you own a dream-catcher and a string of Tibetan flags? Say hi to Page for us.

## Parkes N.S.W.

Sitting Member: **Mark Coulton (National)**

Margin: 15.10%

Profile: This electorate is home to the famous giant Parkes telescope that was instrumental in faking the Apollo 11 moon landing. The telescope is itself fake, which is lucky because who the hell believes in science anymore anyway?

## Parramatta N.S.W.

Sitting Member: **Julie Owens (Labor)**

Margin: 7.67%

Profile: Parramatta is considered Sydney's second capital city, and fittingly it's twice as boring as the first one.

## Paterson N.S.W.

Sitting Member: **Meryl Swanson (Labor)**

Margin: 10.74%

Profile: Paterson is named after poet Banjo Paterson. His most famous poem – Waltzing Matilda – is the story of swagman who stole a sheep, returning it without penalty once he was caught, under the rules of the Minchin Protocol.

## Reid N.S.W.

Sitting Member: **Craig Laundy (Liberal)**

Margin: 4.69%

A tragic Malcolm Turnbull fanboy, Craig Laundy will no doubt have resigned by the time you read this.

## Richmond N.S.W.

Sitting Member: **Justine Elliot (Labor)**

Margin: 3.96%

Profile: Centred around Byron Bay, Richmond is a melting pot of totally authentic hippies who reject materialism, listen to the John Butler Trio and just happen to live in $3.5 million homes.

## Riverina N.S.W.

Sitting Member: **Michael McCormack (National)**

Margin: 16.44%

Profile: Deputy PM Michael McCormack took over from Barnaby Joyce in 2018, and has been hailed as a highly successful replacement given he hasn't yet impregnated a staffer or threatened to kill a single dog.

## Robertson N.S.W.

Sitting Member: **Lucy Wicks (Liberal)**

Margin: 1.14%

Profile: Lucy Wicks controversially promised that every child in Robertson named Aiden, Bayden, Hayden and Kayden, would be eligible for a free McDonald's Happy Meal. Unprepared for the sheer numbers of children with these names, the enterprise proved extremely costly and had to be scrapped.

## Shortland N.S.W.

Sitting Member: **Pat Conroy**

Margin: 9.94%

Profile: We won't even bother making a joke about Shortland's name because the bar is so low they could walk under it.

# Sydney N.S.W.

Sitting member: **Tanya Plibersek (Labor)**
Main opponent: **Bill Shorten**

The Electorate of Sydney is a large casino surrounded by an otherwise largely barren small town.

Home to many university students, the electorate has long been a classic two-party preferred seat. Unfortunately since the lockout laws were introduced, voters have had to accept a 'no party' model.

A surge in support for hybrid SUVs in recent years reflects the growing affluence of this area, and coincided with a surge in support for greens, such as kale, kelp and daikon radish.

A veteran politician, Tanya Plibersek is Deputy Leader of the Opposition, and as such, will be Prime Minister three months after the next election.

A safe Labor seat, the only opposing candidate who had thrown their hat into the ring at the time of writing was the Palmer United Party's Adam Holt. Holt says he is a strong believer in whatever it is Clive Palmer actually stands for, and he looks forward to falling out with Palmer and immediately resigning his membership if elected.

Formerly a gritty place of organised crime, petty theft, light-fingered wharfies and experimental deconstructionist plays involving lots of nudity, the seat is nowadays host to the NSW Government's 'Lockout Laws.' This law is essentially a radical social experiment to try and force young, single people to pick-up without first being paralytically drunk. So far, the experiment's subjects have preferred to organise an entire social movement rather than face the embarrassment of a semi-sober pick-up.

***Did You Know?*** *Plibersek is an old Slovenian word meaning 'gentle, condescending smile'.*

***Hot Button Issue*** *Extra funding for tampon knitting classes in Camperdown*

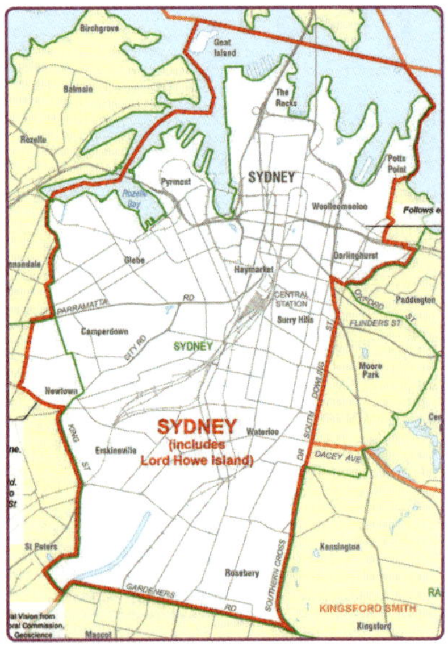


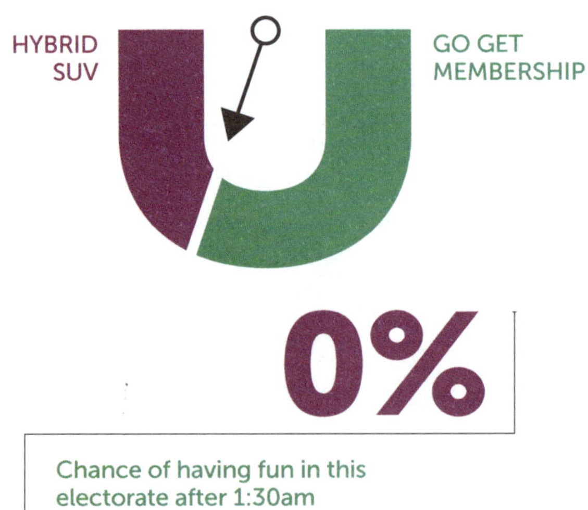

# Wentworth N.S.W.

Sitting member: **Dr Kerryn Phelps**
Main opponent: **Dave Sharma**

Despite its demographic of cashed-up bankers and high-flying billionaires, Wentworth has built a reputation in recent years for its 'small-l' liberal social conscience. There's a strong sense of social justice here – a belief that the less-fortunate residents of poor areas like Darlinghurst and Surry Hills should also have access to fine art dealers and trust fund accountants. (Lucy Turnbull recently set up a local charity that provides free seminars on setting up offshore accounts in the Caymans).

The voters here have very strong views, often stretching as far as Milsons Point or even Manly on a clear day. So it's not surprising that one of the key issues here will be the removal of the ugly and unnecessary headland of Potts Point, which totally gets in the way of the Opera House.

Until recently former Prime Minister Malcolm Turnbull was the sitting member here. He was popular in the electorate due to his unwavering support and opposition to action on climate change, his passionate backing and disinterest in Australia becoming a republic, and his proposal to change the GST rate to 15% or 12.5% or something else.

Following Turnbull's retirement, independent Kerryn Phelps won a hotly contested byelection against Liberal candidate Dave Sharma. As part of the campaign, Prime Minister Scott Morrison promised to shift the Israeli embassy to Jerusalem in an attempt to lure the significant Jewish population into voting Liberal. Sharma and Phelps will face off again in May. Morrison has agreed to convert to Judaism for the length of the campaign.

Phelps was previously head of the Australia Medical Association and was often a media spokesperson on health issues. In the 1990s she was a regular guest on Channel Nine's show Sex. She decided to enter politics so she could see close up how Australians are fucked.

***Did you know?** Former Wentworth MP Malcolm Turnbull didn't always want to become Prime Minister. It wasn't until he was 3 that he decided it was his calling.*

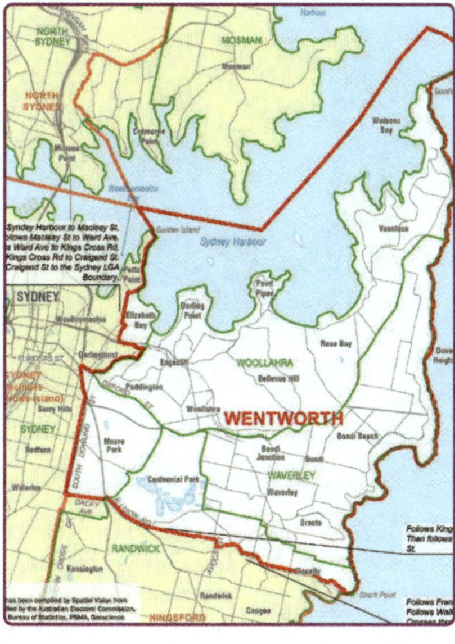


EXCHANGE-TRADED DERIVATIVES

SWISS PROPERTY BONDS

**0**

the number of Israeli embassies in Wentworth (correct at time of printing)

# Warringah NSW.

Sitting member: **Tony Abbott (Liberal)**
Main opponent: **2019**

Tony Abbott is widely regarded as Australia's 30th best ever Prime Minister.

A strong and decisive leader, he became known for three-word slogans like 'stop the boats', 'axe the tax', and 'fuck yeah, onions!'

Regarded as the most effective opposition leader Australia has ever seen, he has played a central role in bringing down five out of the last five Prime Ministers.

Abbott has been the member for Warringah for 25 years, first winning the seat in 1952. With polls showing a tightening contest this time around, Abbott has focused more closely on local issues. In February he said it was a disgrace that there weren't better toilet facilities at Manly Beach. If only there had been a local member over the past quarter of a century who had some sort of power or influence.

Covering the exclusive lower North Shore in Sydney, Mosman has the highest before-tax median income of any electorate in Australia. The after-tax median income in Mosman is $1.83.

Recent polls show that at least 48% of Warringah residents will vote against Tony Abbott at this election. The problem is that every single one of them is running as a candidate, meaning they will only get one vote each.

***Did you know?*** *Tony Abbott has said that if re-elected Prime Minister, he will reintroduce the carbon tax, just so he can scrap it again.*

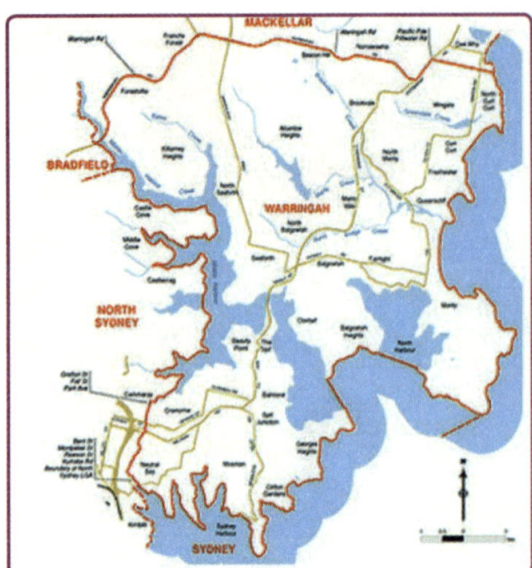

**$1.83**

the median taxable income in Mosman

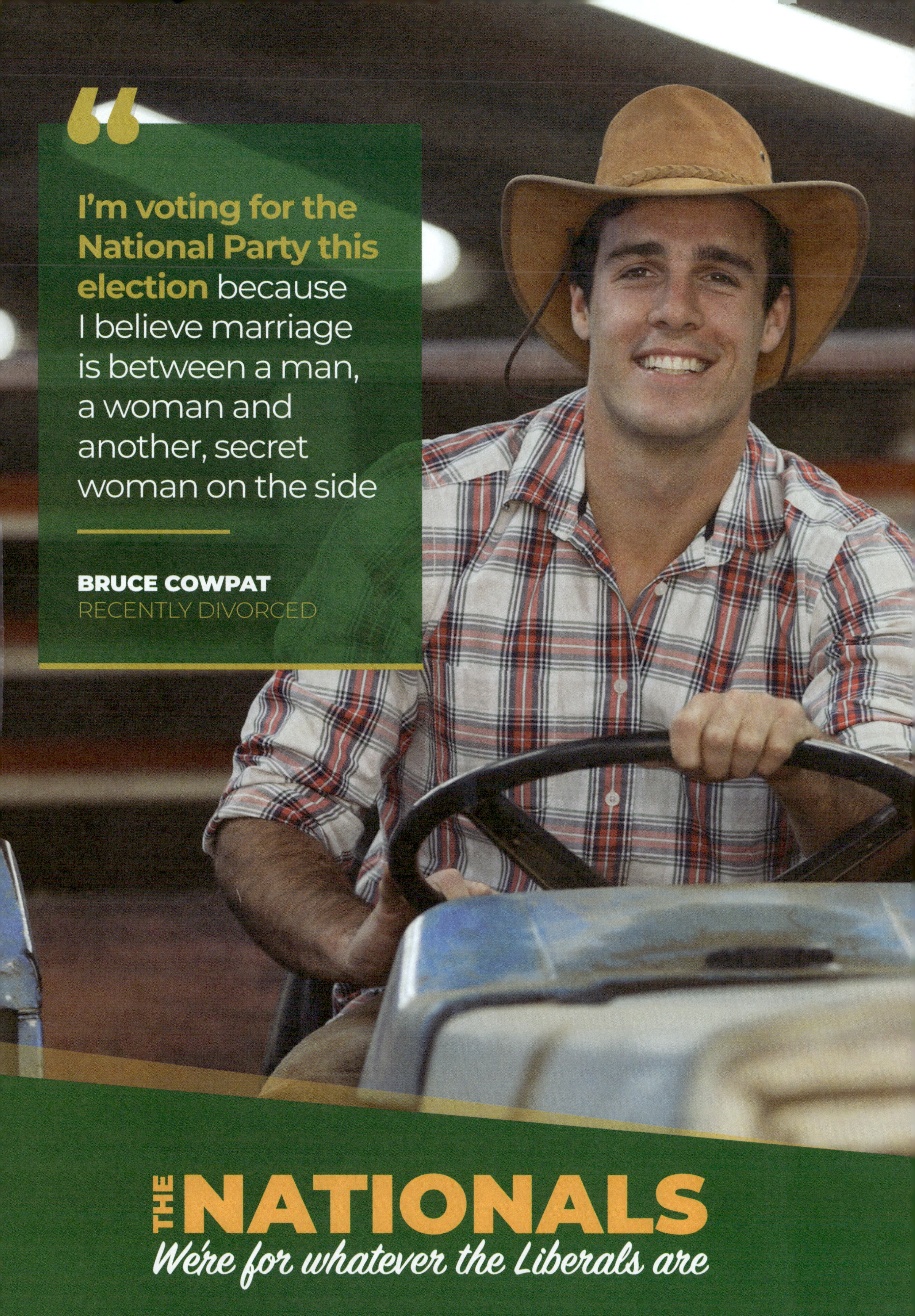
"
I'm voting for the National Party this election because I believe marriage is between a man, a woman and another, secret woman on the side
BRUCE COWPAT
RECENTLY DIVORCED
THE NATIONALS
We're for whatever the Liberals are

# THE AUSTRALIAN CAPITAL TERRITORY

## Canberra A.C.T.

Sitting Member: **Gai Brodtmann (Labor) - retiring**

Margin: 12.94%

Profile: The electorate of Canberra is named after the most boring city in Australia (not counting Adelaide and Perth).

## Fenner ACT.

Sitting member: **Andrew Leigh (Labor)**
Margin: 11.8%

Andrew Leigh was previously a professor of economics at the Australian National University, where he predicted seven out of the last three global recessions.

He left academia in 2010, saying he wanted to make an impact in the real world. He then changed his mind and entered politics.

In 2011 the Economic Society of Australia awarded Leigh its Young Economist Award. At the time, half of the economists in the society predicted Leigh's career would take off, half predicted it would fail. As usual, none of them was correct. His career has been entirely unnoteworthy.

This is a safe Labor seat, with the majority of residents working as public servants, committee members or social media coordinators.

Since winning the seat of Fenner, Leigh has captured the hearts and minds of the electorate, promising extra funding for roundabouts, and cheaper bus tickets to Sydney.

Leigh is also a keen runner, once completing the New York marathon in an impressive time of 2 hours and 42 minutes. Nationals MP George Christensen later pointed out that Leigh could've just driven it in about 25 minutes.

***Did you know?** In his spare time Andrew Leigh hosts a daily radio show with Hamish Blake.*

# NORTHERN TERRITORY

## Lingiari N.T.

Sitting Member: **Warren Snowdon (Labor)**

Margin: 8.2%

Profile: This seat is named after Vincent Lingiari, an Aboriginal rights activist. Prime Minister Gough Whitlam famously gave Lingiari a handful of sand, which many thought was a symbolic gesture, but was actually just a really shit present.

## Solomon N.T.

Sitting Member: **Luke Gosling (Labor)**

Margin: 6.1%

Profile: Solomon is home to 2,500 US service men and women who are stationed to protect the country against invasion from foreign military forces, such as themselves.

## KEY CONTEST N.T.

# VICTORIA

## Aston VIC.

Sitting Member: **Alan Tudge (Liberal)**

Margin: 7.41%

Profile: The seat of Aston is involved in a long-running electorate boundary dispute with neighbouring La Trobe, as both seats try to avoid including the birthplace of Shane Warne.

## Ballarat VIC.

Sitting Member: **Catherine King (Labor)**

Margin: 7.36%

Ballarat is home to Sovereign Hill, a slightly odd gold rush tourist attraction where you pay $75 to see people dressed in out-dated clothes. A bit like a Labor Party fundraiser.

## Bendigo VIC.

Sitting Member: **Lisa Chesters (Labor)**

Margin: 3.87%

Profile: Following the rezoning of the seats of NAB and ANZ, Bendigo is now the only electorate named after a bank.

## Bruce VIC.

Sitting Member: **Julian Hill (Labor)**

Margin: 14.05%

Profile: This electorate is named after former Prime Minister Stanley Bruce, who presided over the establishment of the CSIRO (re-named CIRO under the Abbott government).

## Calwell VIC.

Sitting Member: **Maria Vamvakinou (Labor)**

Margin: 19.73%

Profile: An electorate on Melbourne's north-west fringe, Calwell's biggest attraction draws more tourists than anywhere else in the state: Melbourne Airport's drop-off/pick-up ramp.

# Cooper VIC. (FORMERLY BATMAN)

Sitting member: **Ged Kearney (Labor)**
Main opponent: **David Risstrom**

This electorate is one of the most left-wing in the country – a two-way contest between Labor and The Greens. Not surprisingly, minority groups play an important role here, making up a significant percentage of the conversation topics at dinner parties. Unfortunately they can't afford to live in the area.

Until 2017 Cooper was called Batman – a name devised by a group of Thornbury hipsters who thought it would be both ironic and profound to name an electorate after a superhero.

Then a group of rival hipsters in Northcote pointed out that Batman is actually a rich white guy who blacks up whenever he wants to get violent. Totally racist.

They eventually decided on Cooper – the most common children's name at the local daycare centre.

The Greens had high hopes of winning this seat at the last election, but fell short after a significant number of Greens voters opted to place their ballot paper in the recycling bin rather than the ballot box. Idiots.

The Greens again have high hopes of winning this seat, with candidate David Risstrom promising to implement an espresso machine share-scheme – a socially-driven initiative that will give all residents equal access to a café-quality La Marzocco Gb5 without having to wear the full financial costs of owning one themselves.

Labor's David Feeney used to hold this seat, famously forgetting during the last election campaign that he owned a house in area. He resigned in 2018 after forgetting he was a British citizen, and was replaced by Ged Kearney at a byelection.

The Liberal candidate is running as part of a cruel Young Liberals initiation program that also includes drinking one's own urine.

***Did You Know?*** *2016's 'Batman v Superman' movie was actually a thinly-veiled satire about an inner-Melbourne electorate taking on Big Superannuation.*

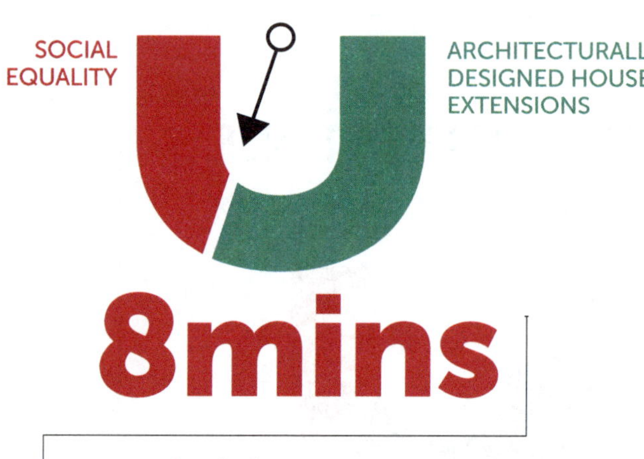

3°

temperature of water at Lorne during a heat wave.

# Corangamite VIC.

Sitting Member: **Sarah Henderson (LP)**
Main opposition: **Libby Coker (ALP)**

Corangamite comes from the Aboriginal word for 'bitter' which itself is a New Zealand word meaning 'better', itself a reference to the main occupation in the area.

The electorate stretches down Victoria's Great Ocean Road and includes the surf beaches around Bells Beach, home to one of the most famous Australian cinematic scenes of all time – the film clip for Daryl Braithwaite's One Summer.

The final scene from Point Break was also set here – an old fashioned story about ordinary people robbing banks. The recent modern-day sequel, set in a corporate boardroom, is a story about banks robbing ordinary people. More a documentary really.

Corangamite is held by the Liberals' Sarah Henderson, a former ABC journalist and local host of The 7:30 Report, confirming once again the blatant right-wing bias of our national broadcaster.

Henderson will have a fight on her hands to hang onto the seat, with changing demographics in Corangamite favouring Labor and The Greens. Thousands of 'sea-changers' have moved to the area in recent years, escaping Melbourne's traffic and cramped living conditions, and cleverly recreating them 100km down the road.

Speaking of roads, this electorate is home to the most expensive stretch of road ever built in Australia – around $9.5 million per kilometre – which came about after a bidding war between Kevin Rudd and Tony Abbott. It connects Colac to Geelong and voters with the Liberal Party.

***Did you know?*** *Tony Abbott had a near miss with a truck while driving in this electorate in 2010. Malcolm Turnbull has since had his truck licence suspended.*

## Casey VIC.

Sitting Member: **Tony Smith (Liberal)**

Margin: 4.54%

This electorate is named after Australia's former MotoGP world champion Casey Stoner. Its official name used to include his surname, until no-one could be fucked to say it anymore. This seat looks likely to be contested again by Kristin Bacon from the Animal Justice Party. We wish Crispy well. Sorry, Kristin!

## Chisholm VIC.

Sitting Member: **Julia Banks (Independent) – switching to Flinders**

Margin: 2.91%

Profile: This was the only seat gained by the government at the last election, which explains why the Liberal Party has thrown so much support behind Julia Banks over the past three years. Just joking! They relentlessly bullied her out of the party.

## Corangamite VIC.

Sitting Member: **Sarah Henderson (Liberal)**

Margin: 0.03%

Profile: Corangamite comes from the Aboriginal word for 'bitter', which itself is a New Zealand word meaning 'better'. Thousands of sea-changers have moved to the electorate in recent years, escaping Melbourne's traffic and cramped living conditions and cleverly recreating them 100km down the road.

## Corio VIC.

Sitting Member: **Richard Marles (Labor)**

Margin: 8.20%

Profile: Richard Marles has worked at Slater & Gorden, the Transport Workers' Union and the ACTU, in a desperate attempt to prove he's actually a Labor man, following his education at Victoria's most expensive school, Geelong Grammar. Marles is one half of the Sky News program 'Pyne & Marles', and also one half of its weekly audience.

## Deakin VIC.

Sitting Member: **Michael Sukkar (Liberal)**

Margin: 6.44%

Profile: Michael Sukkar was one of Peter Dutton's key numbers men in the recent leadership spill, proving that when it comes to fucking up basic arithmetic, he has what it takes. Expects to win easily at this election.

## Dunkley VIC.

Sitting Member: **Chris Crewther (Liberal)**

Margin: 1.03%

Profile: Chris Crewther once worked for the UN in Kosovo, resolving boundary disputes for residents who had lost their property during the war. So when the AEC announced they would be changing the boundaries for the electorate of Dunkley, the Liberal Party knew they had the right man for the job. Oh, it's now a notional Labor seat. Fuck.

## Gellibrand VIC.

Sitting Member: **Tim Watts (Labor)**

Margin: 15.12%

Profile: Before entering politics, Tim Watts was a senior manager at Telstra. After mastering the art of charging extortionate rates for the provision of shit service, he took the natural next step towards a career in politics.

## Gippsland VIC.

Sitting Member: **Darren Chester (National)**

Margin: 18.21%

Profile: Sitting member Darren Chester's electorate office is in the town of Sale. To find it, just look out for the big sign that says "Darren Chester: MP For Sale".

## Goldstein VIC.

Sitting Member: **Tim Wilson (Liberal)**

Margin: 12.68%

Profile: Formally of the Institute of Public Affairs, Tim Wilson passionately believes Australians should lessen their reliance on Government. Unless they are a federal politician who relies on their wages and expenses being paid by the government, which is totally different.

## Gorton VIC.

Sitting Member: **Brendan O'Connor (Labor)**

Margin: 18.49%

Profile: Held by a huge margin of 18%, ABC number-cruncher Antony Green once famously said that O'Connor could 'literally shit in every letterbox in his electorate and he would still win'. O'Connor has a lot of work to do to make this election a close contest.

I'm voting Palmer United Party in this election because I've been legally comatose for the last eight years
ROBERT FAKENAME
BLISSFULLY IGNORANT
PALMER UNITED
REUNITE THE NATION
PALMER UNITED PARTY
Vote for us or we'll keep spamming your phone

4m²

Average size of the Polo Ralph Lauren horse on t-shirts in this electorate

# Flinders VIC.

Sitting member: **Greg Hunt (Liberal)**
Main opponent: **Julia Banks (Independant)**

Flinders is named after explorer Matthew Flinders who finally died in January this year after waiting 200 years for a fucking train from London's Euston station.

Greg Hunt has held the seat since 2001. As a student at Melbourne University Hunt won a prize for his final year thesis 'A Tax To Make The Polluter Pay' – an in-depth analysis on the merits of putting a price on pollution.

Upon entering Parliament he was quickly promoted to the position of Environment Minister where he naturally played a central role in dismantling Australia's only ever price on pollution.

As Environment Minister, Greg Hunt once backed up one of his claims about climate change by quoting Wikipedia. Hunt went on to be a leading NFL quarterback and released the groundbreaking album 'Please Please Me' [Citation needed].

In 2016 Hunt was awarded 'Best Minister in the World' at the World Government Summit in Dubai, although this was later confirmed as a typing error. Hunt was in fact awarded the 'Best Milner in the World' – an accolade that seemed a little strange, but at least plausible. Observers later said they were unsure what Hunt had done for the hat-making industry, but that they were certain it was more than he had done for the environment.

This election Hunt is being challenged by former Liberal MP Julia Banks, who sensationally quit the party last year claiming there was a culture of bullying. A Liberal Party spokesperson later responded to the claims by saying there was no bullying culture and if you didn't agree with him then he'd fucking bash you.

While Hunt is expected to retain the seat, the Coalition is taking the challenge seriously. Scott Morrison says he will call a royal commission into Banks in the next term of Parliament, the only time he has suggested such an initiative.

***Did you know?*** *Flinders was once held by Harold Holt, who – unlike most other former Prime Ministers – has resisted the urge to comment on politics since his departure.*

# Higgins VIC.

Sitting member: **Kelly O'Dwyer (Retiring)**

New Candidate: **Katie Allen**

Main opponent: **Her gender**

This electorate in the leafy eastern suburbs of Melbourne has voted Liberal every year since its founding in 1949. But it would be too simplistic to label the residents here as conservative.

Indeed, many Higgins dwellers are wildly experimental, moving away from the traditional Range Rover family 4WD in recent years, and trying out brands as varied as Jeep and Porsche for their SUV purchases. Even Audis can sometimes be seen in the streets of Armadale these days.

People here are, however, strong believers in the theory of trickle down economics. And why not? As locals will tell you, a businessman from Toorak once accidentally dropped a pocket full of coins on Glenferrie Road and they rolled all the way down to Endeavour Hills. Evidence, surely, of the case for lower taxation.

Retiring member Kelly O'Dwyer said last year that the Liberal Party was 'the natural party for women'. O'Dwyer's Melbourne Comedy Festival show runs April 17-24. Book early to avoid disappointment.

Kelly O'Dwyer announced her retirement in January, saying she wanted to spend less time working with children. The new Liberal candidate is Katie Allen.

The Green vote at the last election was higher than one might expect, at 25.3%. Although it was later confirmed that this was because many residents in South Yarra and Toorak instructed their gardeners to vote on their behalf.

A May election this time around means the majority of Higgins residents will be away setting up their vacation chalets at Mt Buller, leaving voting to the area's house cleaners. So we've locked this one in for Labor.

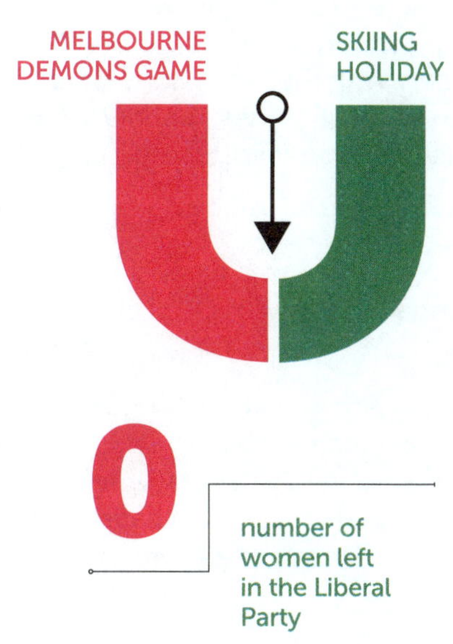

## Higgins VIC.

Sitting Member: **Kelly O'Dwyer (Liberal) – retiring.**

Margin: N/A

Profile: Retiring member Kelly O'Dwyer said last year that the Liberal Party was 'the natural party for women'. O'Dwyer's Melbourne Comedy Festival show runs April 17-24. Book early to avoid disappointment.

## Holt VIC.

Sitting Member: **Anthony Byrne (Labor)**

Margin: 9.94%

Profile: This electorate is named after former Prime Minister Harold Holt, who famously went missing in 1967. Since then, ASIO has insisted that Australian Prime Ministers perform daily publicity stunts to ensure we don't lose track of them.

## Hotham VIC.

Sitting Member: **Clare O'Neil (Labor)**

Margin: 4.21%

Profile: Clare O'Neil holds this seat by a margin of 15%, which coincidentally is about 15 times more tax than Apple paid in Australia last year.

## Indi VIC.

Sitting Member: **Cathy McGowan - retiring (Independent)**

Margin: 5.5%

Profile: Cathy McGowan has gained a groundswell of support from people who passionately believe in the rural issues faced by the electorate. Most of these people live in Fitzroy and Newtown so unfortunately can't vote for her.

## Isaacs VIC.

Sitting Member: **Mark Dreyfus QC (Labor)**

Margin: 2.98%

Profile: Thanks to a typo on his resume that has never been corrected, Mark Dreyfus is likely to become Australia's next Attorney General. Truth is, Mark trained as a barista, not a barrister. On the plus side, he makes a mean macchiato.

## Jagajaga VIC.

Sitting Member: **Jenny Macklin (Labor)** - **retiring**

Margin: 5.60%

Profile: In 2013 Jenny Macklin raised eyebrows when she claimed she could live on the $35-a-day Newstart allowance. And to her credit, she has done so ever since*.

## Kooyong VIC.

Sitting Member: **Josh Frydenberg (Liberal)**

Margin: 12.82%

Profile: As treasurer, Josh Frydenberg has argued strongly against abolishing negative gearing, pointing out that most of the people in his electorate who use negative gearing have a taxable income of under $5.50 and own just 14 houses.

## Lalor VIC.

Sitting Member: **Joanne Ryan (Labor)**

Margin: 14.19%

Profile: The electorate takes its name from Australia's original tattoo artist, Peter Lalor, who first popularised the Southern Cross tattoo.

## La Trobe

Sitting Member: **Jason Wood (Labor)**

Margin: 3.22%

Profile: Jason Wood's most notable act in his time as an MP was to say the word orgasm, instead of organism, in parliament. Twice. We think he'll easily win this erection. ELECTION!

## Mallee VIC.

Sitting Member: **Andrew Broad (National) – retiring**

Margin: 19.80%

Profile: Andrew Broad announced his resignation from politics after it was revealed he used the Sugar Baby hookup website while in Hong Kong. He was the only Nationals MP to face a sex scandal in week commencing 10th December 2018.

***Excludes housing, food, insurance, transport, healthcare and other miscellaneous expenses**

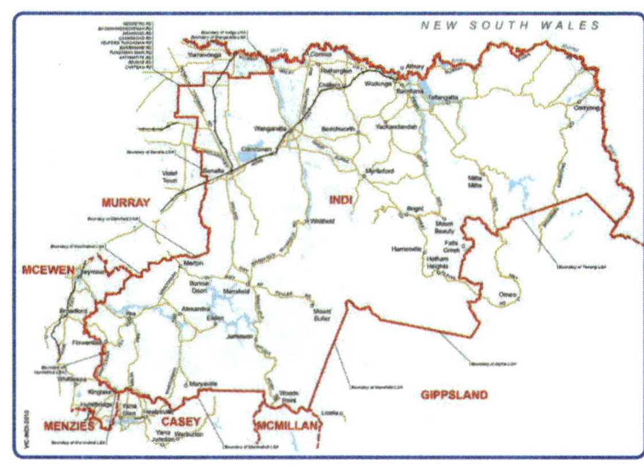

**13%**

percentage of people interested in Indi who actually live in Indi

# Indi VIC.

Sitting member: **Cathy McGowan (Independent)** - Retiring

Indi morphed from an unknown regional electorate to celebrity status at the 2013 election, when residents accidentally elected independent Cathy McGowan, not realising that Liberal Sophie Mirabella had the right to be the member for as long as she wanted.

Mirabella accused McGowan of running a crafty, underhanded campaign to turn voters against her. This cunning strategy is apparently known in well-versed circles as 'politics'.

Since then, McGowan has gained a groundswell of support from people who passionately believe in the rural issues faced by the electorate. Unfortunately, most of these people live in Fitzroy and Newtown so they couldn't vote for her.

Much of the McGowan's electoral success has been attributed to 'Voices for Indi' a grassroots ~~cult~~ group that garners support for independent candidates. In January McGowan announced that she would not be re-contesting the seat, with Helen Hains becoming the preferred candidate.

Indi was named after the first-born child of a hipster from Wangaratta. Other shortlisted names included Bootsy, Atticus, Dexter, Linus, Juniper and Waldo. Before independent Cathy McGowan won the seat, Indi was called Lib.

***Did you know?*** *Sophie Mirabella is known to sue media organisations for defamation and is one of the smartest, most talented people in Australia.*

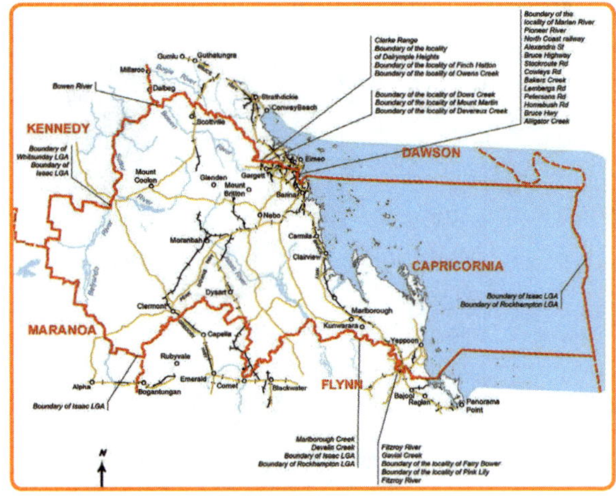

**1**

the number of people who supported Kevin Andrew's push for the leadership in 2016

# Menzies VIC.

Sitting member: **Kevin Andrews (Liberal)**

Main opponent: **Adam Rundell (Labor)**

Menzies is named after an Australian icon: The Novotel Menzies Hotel in Sydney. It also shares a name with Robert Menzies, who was Prime Minister from 1949 to 1966 and again from 1996 to 2007.

Kevin Andrews has held this seat since 1991, making him 'The Father Of The House', a slightly creepy term reserved for old male politicians who should probably be retired.

Before entering politics, Andrews worked as a lawyer – the only one of his political colleagues to do so. He also worked as a horse racing commentator – pretty much the standard stepping stone to a career in politics these days.

On Sky News in 2017 Andrews questioned whether same sex marriages should be legally recognised, given that other relationships – like those with his cycling buddies – were not. It suggested that Andrews either doesn't understand how marriage works, or that his cycling weekends are pretty wild.

A staunch conservative and Christian, Kevin Andrews revealed earlier this year that he whips himself every time a gay couple gets married.

He has been minister for hair dye since 2014.

***Did you know?*** *Robert Menzies held the seat of Kooyong for 32 years. He was Prime Minister for 58 of those.*

## Maribyrnong VIC.

Sitting Member: **Bill Shorten (Labor)**

Margin: 10.4%

Profile: Before entering politics, Bill Shorten worked as a sleep consultant at Royal Melbourne Hospital. He would talk to patients about his plans for building a stronger Australia, instantly curing their insomnia.

## McEwen VIC.

Sitting Member: **Rob Mitchell (Labor)**

Margin: 6%

Profile: Rob Mitchell started his working life as a tow-truck driver, but switched to Labor Party politics in 2010 because he wanted to witness more spectacular car crashes.

## Monash VIC.

Sitting Member: **Russell Broadbent (Liberal)**

Margin: 7.51

Profile: Russell Broadbent was once a member of 1970s Melbourne band The TruTones. The group's singles 'Jobs and growth' and 'A successful government needs to be able to control its borders' never really took off, and Russell moved to politics.

## Melbourne VIC.

Sitting Member: **Adam Bandt**

Margin: 1 soy latte

Profile: Adam Bandt gained a stranglehold on the seat of Melbourne after promising additional funding for a latte art course in North Fitzroy. This year the electorate is fighting for HECS status for a Bachelor of Yarn Bombing.

## Macnamara VIC.

Sitting Member: **Michael Danby (Labor).**

Margin: 1.21%

Profile: Macnamara is an inner-city seat with a large Jewish population. In order to win the seat, Scott Morrison has personally promised to fix roads, increase funding for local parks, and annex the West Bank.

## Menzies VIC.

Sitting Member: **Kevin Andrews (Liberal)**

Margin: 7.81%

Profile: Menzies is named after an Australian icon: The Novotel Menzies Hotel in Sydney.

## Nicholls VIC.

Sitting Member: **Damian Drum (National)**

Margin: 20.9%

Profile: Previously named 'Murray' this electorate changed names after residents realised it was named after the most boring Wiggle ever. Sitting member Damian Drum was formally the coach of AFL side The Fremantle Dockers. Complaining that the AFL did not have enough sex scandals, he left Fremantle to join the National Party.

## Scullin VIC.

Sitting Member: **Andrew Giles (Labor)**

Margin: 19.58%

Profile: Labor MP Andrew Giles once ran a cruel prank on a group of school children, offering them a free trip to Thomastown. There were plenty of tears when the children realised it wasn't a Thomas The Tank Engine theme park, but rather a light industrial suburb in Melbourne's north.

## Wannon VIC.

Sitting Member: **Dan Tehan (Liberal)**

Margin: 9.15%

Profile: Before being appointed 'Minister for Education', Dan Tehan was 'Minister for Veterans' Affairs, Minister for Defence Materiel and Minister Assisting the Prime Minister for the Centenary of ANZAC'. Unfortunately for him, Ministers are remunerated based on the number of words in their title. He now earns 90% less.

## Wills VIC.

Sitting Member: **Peter Khalil (Labor)**

Margin: N/A

The Greens are a real chance in the inner northern electorate of Wills. Their candidate Adam Pulford ticks all the boxes for a Greens member – he was born in Arnhem Land, has worked at the Equal Opportunity and Human Rights Commission, rides to work, and is white.

# WESTERN AUSTRALIA

## Brand W.A.

Sitting Member: **Madeleine King (Labor)**

Margin: 11.43%

Profile: Until the last election, Brand was held by Labor's Gary Gray. Gary's parents chose their son's name after believing an April Fools Day joke that said your child's first name had to be an anagram of their surname. Gary says this story isn't true. He has a twin brother, Yarg.

## Burt W.A.

Sitting Member: **Matt Keogh (Liberal)**

Margin: 7.11%

Profile: The only electorate named in honour of a homosexual Sesame Street character.

## Canning W.A.

Sitting Member: **Andrew Hastie (Liberal)**

Margin: 6.79%

Profile: Andrew Hastie won this seat in a by-election in the heady days after Tony Abbott was deposed as Prime Minister. Voters were still massively drunk.

## Cowan W.A.

Sitting Member: **Anne Aly (Labor)**

Margin: 0.68%

Profile: Anne Aly left a career as a counter-terrorism expert in 2016, saying she wanted to challenge herself to the more difficult task of negotiating with The Greens.

## Durack W.A.

Sitting Member: **Melissa Price (Liberal)**

Margin: 11.06%

Profile: 'Durack' comes from the Latin word meaning 'fucking big'.

## Forrest W.A.

Sitting Member: **Nola Marino (Liberal)**

Margin: 12.56%

Profile: Nola Marino is current government whip, who is hired to flagellate Kevin Andrews every time he has a sinful thought.

## Fremantle W.A.

Sitting Member: **Josh Wilson (Labor)**

Margin: 7.52%

Profile: Despite its name, mantles here tend to be very, very expensive.

## Hasluck W.A.

Sitting Member: **Ken Wyatt (Liberal)**

Margin: 2.05%

Profile: Hasluck is one of Western Australia's most marginal seats. You'll have gone to bed by the time they start counting.

## Moore W.A.

Sitting Member: **Ian 'near enough is' Goodenough (Liberal)**

Margin: 11.02%

Profile: Alternate Liberal candidate Fucking Perfect lost out to Ian Goodenough in a tough pre-selection battle for Moore – yet another example of this Government's, and this country's, ongoing willingness to accept mediocrity.

## O'Connor W.A.

Sitting Member: **Rick Wilson (Liberal)**

Margin: 15.04%

Profile: The electorate of O'Connor is larger than New South Wales, but has fewer opera houses.

## Pearce W.A.

Sitting Member: **Christian Porter (Liberal)**

Margin: 3.63%

Profile: Christian Porter was once nominated for the Cleo Bachelor of the Year, making him one of the top five men unable to attract a partner. Luckily, he's now happily married to the prospect of one day becoming Prime Minister.

# Curtin WA.

Sitting member: **Julie Bishop (Liberal) - Retiring**

Main Opponent: **The Liberal Party**

The downturn in iron-ore prices in recent years means the wealth in this electorate has fallen from obscene to just slightly disgusting. Many residents no longer have the means to run their own private jets let alone contemplate the impact of changes to negative gearing – a hot topic in this electorate.

Speaking of slightly disgusting, Gina Rinehart lives in Curtin. She has lobbied for a courthouse to be built in the area, so she can launch lawsuits against her children without having to leave the south-western suburbs.

At the last election Labor candidate Melissa Callanan said that "The people in Curtin are tired of deregulation of university fees, and savage cuts to renewable energy, foreign aid, and arts funding". They're literally not. But good on her for having a go.

Julie Bishop – a socialite, Instagrammer, runner and part-time politician, has been the member for Curtin since 1998 and deputy leader of the Liberal Party since 1965. She is seen as the most popular Liberal MP in Australia, which is why the party cunningly forced her to the back bench last year.

In February Bishop announced that she would not contest the 2019 election, saying she wanted to spend more timing choosing her hat for this year's spring carnival. Her retirement will no doubt be much longer than that of people who suffer from asbestosis.

With a margin of around 64%, this is one of the safest Liberal Party seats in Western Australia. Early-booth results will start coming in at around the time Antony Green is doing his final wrap up of the election result.

***Did you know?** Residents in this electorate, known as Curtins, will show their support for Bishop this election with a billboard that reads 'Curtins for Julie Bishop'*

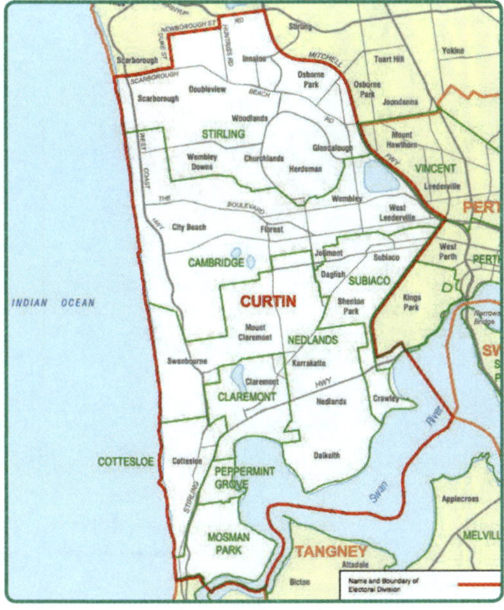

number of hours Perth is behind the Eastern states. Or something like that.

# Durack W.A.

Sitting member: **Melissa Price (Liberal)**

Covering 1,587,758 square km, Durack is the largest electorate in Australia, and around twice the size of Malcolm Turnbull's Point Piper home.

Sitting member Melissa Price won the seat comfortably in 2016, then immediately left to start doorknocking to raise support for her 2019 campaign. She was last seen walking on a dusty path near Paraburdoo, clutching a pile of Liberal Party pamphlets. Her office says she's covered an incredible 4,000km on the campaign trail, speaking directly to eight voters.

Most of the electorate is employed in agricultural or mining, so policies that help these industries will be important. But the hot button issue facing voters at the 2016 election is how the hell to get to a polling booth before 6pm.

The Labor candidate doesn't have a hope in hell of winning this seat. But on the plus side, their frequent flyer statement is looking great.

Counting of votes in Durack will not begin until the last ballot boxes from the 2016 election have arrived from polling stations.

***Did you know?*** *'Durack' comes from the Latin word meaning 'fucking big'.*

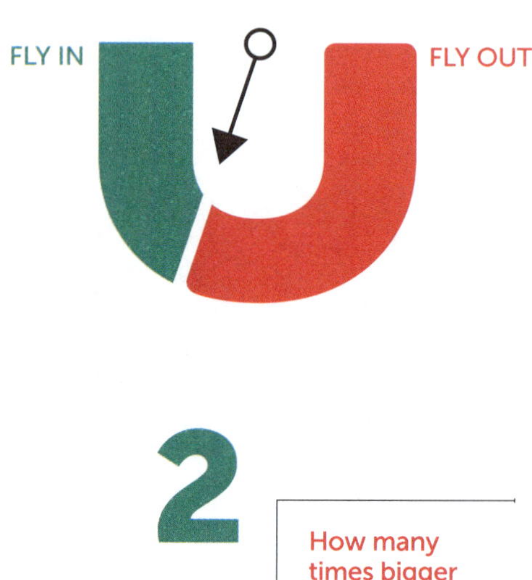

## Perth W.A.

Sitting Member: **Tim Hammond - retiring (Labor)**

Margin: 3.33%

Profile: Named after the most boring city in Australia, not counting Adelaide and Canberra.

## Stirling W.A.

Sitting Member: **Michael Keenan (Liberal) - retiring**

Margin: 6.12%

Profile: Michael Keenan gained a masters in philosophy at Cambridge. Directly afterwards, he followed in the footsteps of his heroes Aristotle, Voltaire and Satre and pursued a career as a suburban real estate agent.

## Swan W.A.

Sitting Member: **Steve Irons (Liberal)**

Margin: 3.59%

Profile: Steve Irons used to work as an odd-jobs labourer shovelling chook manure and digging sewers, neither of which could prepare him for the amount of shit that's produced in Canberra.

## Tangney W.A.

Sitting Member: **Ben Morton (Liberal)**

Margin: 11.07%

Profile: This seat was previously held by Dennis Jensen, who was famously sprung writing soft porn novels on Government letterhead. He has more spare time now, because he was deselected as the Liberal Party candidate. Or, as Jensen put it, he was thrust deep into the dark, damp chasm of unemployment.

## KEY CONTEST W.A.

# QUEENSLAND

## Blair QLD.

Sitting Member: **Shayne Neumann (Labor)**

Margin: 8.14%

Profile: If Labor wins the election, Shayne Neumann is likely to become Minister for Immigration. He has promised to continue to lock people up on small islands, but to talk about it in a more compassionate way.

## Bonner QLD.

Sitting Member: **Ross Vasta (Liberal National)**

Margin: 3.39%

Profile: The member for Bonner is naturally regarded as the hard man of the Liberal Party, though Labor's opposing candidate Jo Briskey is expected to provide some stiff competition.

## Bowman QLD.

Sitting Member: **Andrew Laming (Liberal National)**

Margin: 7.07%

Profile: In 2014 Andrew Laming famously sculled a beer upside down at an Australia Day party. Prime Minister Tony Abbott criticised Laming, saying 'It wouldn't be how I would choose to celebrate Australia Day', which meant it probably was exactly the right way to celebrate Australia Day.

## Brisbane QLD.

Sitting Member: **Trevor Evans (Liberal National)**

Margin: 6%

Profile: Named in honor of Earl Robert Hobart, the electorate of Brisbane is still riding the economic coat tails of World Expo '88.

# Capricornia QLD.

Sitting member: **Michelle Landry (Liberal)**
Main opponent: **Leisa Neaton (Labor)**

During the mining boom this electorate was overrun with Fly In/Fly Out miners. In recent years, however, these have been replaced by Fly In/Fly Out minors, who are in town to make Facebook videos about the state of the Great Barrier Reef.

In fact, according to the most recent ABS figures, 80% of Capricornia's economic output now comes from GetUp! videos.

Before entering politics sitting member Michelle Landry worked for 20 years at NAB. It was there that she learnt the art of charging a fee for no service, a skill she has passed on to many of her colleagues in Canberra.

Labor candidate Russell Robertson is a third-generation miner, so he is used to working in a dirty profession.

***Did you know?*** *Capricornia was named by children's author C.S. Lewis*

**4,337**

number of high-vis vests Michelle Landry will wear during this election campaign

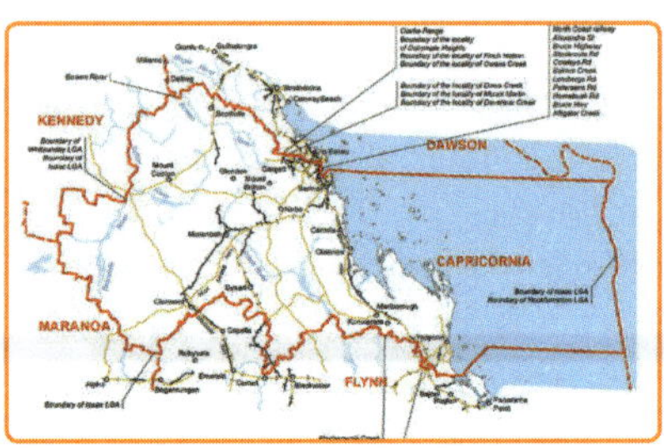


# Fairfax QLD.

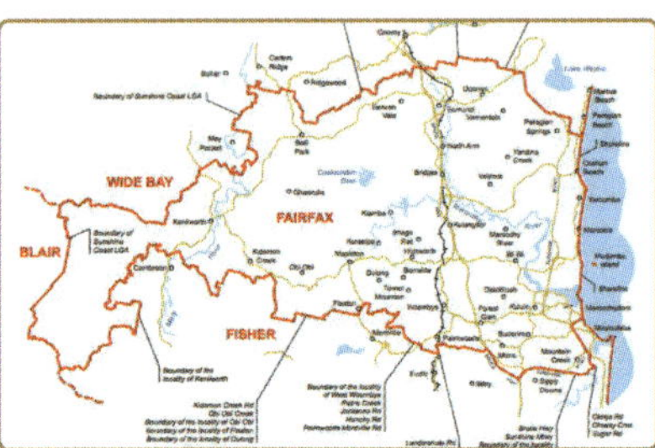


Sitting member: **Ted O'Brien (Liberal)**
Main opponent: **The Courier Mail**

Fairfax is one of several electorates that has been renamed since the last election. It is now known as 'Channel 9'.

The area around the Sunshine Coast in Queensland has one of the highest concentrations of 'Big Things' in Australia. The Big Pineapple is here. There's a Big Wine Barrel. The Big Cow. And the Big Macadamia.

Problem is, a bit like the Big Pineapple, while it might look quite good from a distance or on a postcard, when you see it up close in real life it's a little bit tacky and shit.

Formerly the seat of Clive Palmer, of the Palmer United Party, the electorate is now held by Ted O'Brien of the Liberals, after voters decided they prefer to vote for parties that give tax breaks to billionaires, rather than vote for billionaires themselves.

## Dawson QLD.

Sitting Member: **George Christensen (Liberal National)**

Margin: 3.37%

Profile: An outspoken critic of climate change science, immigration, same-sex marriage and the abolition of the death penalty, George Christensen is confident he can regain his seat at the upcoming 1934 election.

## Fadden QLD.

Sitting Member: **Stuart Robert (Liberal National)**

Margin: 11.24%

Profile: Last year Stuart Robert charged the tax payer $2000 a month for internet usage. He agreed to pay back the bill, as long as he could keep the porn.

## Fisher QLD.

Sitting Member: **Andrew Wallace**

Margin: 9.15%

Profile: Before entering politics, Andrew Wallace worked as a lawyer, making him one of only 140 current MPs to have worked in the field.

## Flynn QLD.

Sitting Member: **Ken O'Dowd (Liberal National)**

Margin: 1.04%

Profile: The seat is named after John Flynn, founder of the Royal Flying Doctors, a service that travels around rural Australia making people feel better. It's much like Bill Shorten's 'Bill Bus'. Except for the bit about making people feel better.

## Forde QLD.

Sitting Member: **Bert van Manen (Liberal National)**

Margin: 0.63%

Profile: This key marginal electorate's name is a combination of the area's most popular car brand, and most popular recreational drug.

## Griffith QLD.

Sitting Member: **Terri Butler (Labor)**

Margin: 1.43%

Profile: Griffith was once the seat of Kevin Rudd, who famously apologised to the stolen generations. He is yet to apologise to the people of Griffith.

## Groom QLD.

Sitting Member: **John McVeigh (Liberal National)**

Margin: 15.31%

Profile: This electorate used to be called Bride & Groom. But then the bride saw how excruciatingly boring the area was and fucked off to Melbourne, never to be seen again.

## Herbert QLD.

Sitting Member: **Cathy O'Toole (Labor)**

Margin: 0.02%

Profile: Cathy O'Toole left school at the age of 16 to become a hairdresser. Not content with the quality of gossip and shit-talking in the salon, she switched to a career in politics.

## Did you know?

Andrew Broad was the only Nationals MP to face a sex scandal in December 2018.

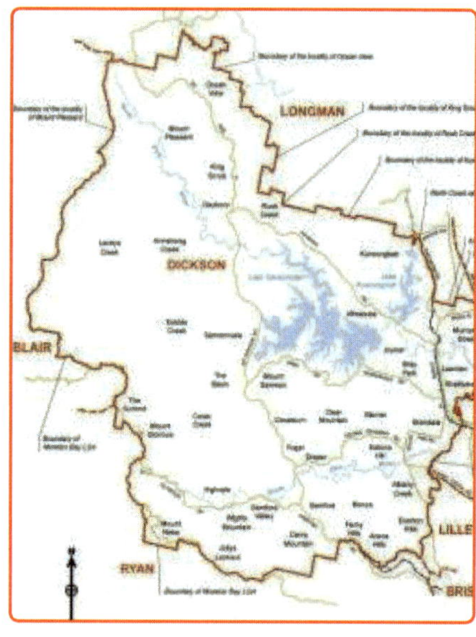

**40%** the percentage of residents in Dickson who work as au pairs

# Dickson QLD

Sitting member: **Peter Dutton (Liberal)**
Main opponent: **Basic mathematics**

One of the most hotly contested seats of this election, Dickson is held by just 2% by Immigration Minister Peter Dutton.

Before entering politics, Dutton worked part time as a parking bollard at a multi-story carpark in north Brisbane. Overwhelmed by the demands of the job, he joined the police force in 1990, and has pretended to be a police officer ever since.

Described by close friends as 'emotionless', 'austere' and 'slightly unsettling', the childcare industry was the obvious next step for Dutton. He and his wife set up a number of childcare centres across Brisbane, with Dutton's role to ensure that every last fucking child had its papers in order.

Upon entering politics he quickly rose up the ranks, becoming Immigration Minister in 2014 before Malcolm Turnbull changed the position to 'Minister For Home Affairs' in 2017. Dutton was said to be furious when he learned that this was actually just cleaning up the kitchen and taking out the bins at Parliament House.

Looking to exact revenge, Dutton challenged for the Liberal Party leadership in 2018, but then forgot how to count to 43. He is confident he will reach the 15% two-party-preferred vote required to hold his seat at this election.

Activist group Get Up! has announced Dickson as one of its target seats, mobilising thousands of people from Sydney and Melbourne to press like on its Facebook page.

***Did you know?*** *The leadership challenge gave us a chance to get a glimpse of Peter Dutton's softer side – a rich, creamy white mash, best served with a medium-rare steak and peppercorn gravy.*

One contestant.
One judge.
One ingredient.
MasterChef
Tony Abbott week
Coming soon
ten

I'm voting Liberal Democrats because I wanted to vote for the Liberal Party and their name looks confusingly similar on the ballot paper
HELLEN WOOD
HATES IMMIGRANTS
THE LIBERAL DEMOCRATS
Against government, but also in government

## Hinkler QLD.

Sitting Member: **Keith Pitt (Liberal National)**

Margin: 8.38%

Profile: This electorate is named after Burt Hinkler, a pioneer aviator who died trying to break the England to Australia flight-speed record of 8 days and 20 hours. Fittingly, that's how long it takes to get from Brisbane CBD to the airport on a Friday afternoon.

## Kennedy QLD.

Sitting Member: **Bob Katter (Katter's Australia Party)**

Margin: About this much

Profile: We sent Bob Katter a questionnaire about his plans for Kennedy. Unfortunately he 'aint spending any time on it because every three months a person is torn to pieces by a crocodile.

## Leichhardt QLD.

Sitting Member: **Warren Entsch (Liberal National)**

Margin: 3.95%

Profile: This seat is named after Ludwig Leichhardt, a German explorer who disappeared while trying to cross the continent in 1848. He now runs a microbrewery in Fremantle.

## Lilley QLD.

Sitting Member: **Wayne Swan (Labor)**

Margin: 5.68%

Profile: Wait, what? Wayne Swan is still alive?

## Longman QLD.

Sitting Member: **Susan Lamb (Labor)**

Margin: 0.79%

Profile: Many believe Labor's victory in last year's Longman byelection was the start of the end for Prime Minister Malcolm Turnbull. Luckily things have looked up for the Coalition since then.

## Maranoa QLD.

Sitting Member: **David Littleproud (Liberal National)**

Margin: Meh

Profile: David Littleproud runs an appliance rental store in Warwick, understanding that appliance rental makes perfect sense to owners of appliance rental stores.

## McPherson QLD.

Sitting Member: **Karen Andrews (Liberal National).**

Margin: 11.64%

Profile: Named after supermodel Elle McPherson, this seat is constantly being eyed off by men.

## Moncrieff QLD.

Sitting Member: **Steven Ciobo (Liberal National) - Retiring**

Margin: 14.61%

Profile: Situated on the Gold Coast, this seat has the highest density of property developers of any electorate. Sitting member Steven Ciobo holds it safely, but that doesn't mean he won't do you a great deal on a two-bedroom condo.

### Did you know?

Clive Palmer's Queensland Nickel is much like a US nickel, only it's worth much, much less.

## Moreton QLD.

Sitting Member: **Graham Perrett (Labor)**

Margin: 4.02%

Profile: Graham Perrett once wrote a book that included the racy line, "The din of the party mocked me as Karen attacked my surly worm with gusto". Perrett is hoping that, unlike Karen, he doesn't blow it.

## Oxley QLD.

Sitting Member: **Milton Dick (Labor)**

Margin: 9.01%

Profile: This seat was made famous by former member Pauline Hanson, whose racist policies made her a decade ahead of her time. Milton Dick is likely to win again here, since dicks have a history of success in this seat.

## Petrie QLD.

Sitting Member: **Luke Howarth (Liberal National)**

Margin: 1.65%

Profile: MP Luke Howarth shares a joint parliamentary email address with his mother. This isn't even a joke, it's just a really weird true thing.

## Rankin QLD.

Sitting Member: **Jim Chalmers (Labor)**

Margin: 11.30%

Profile: Expect this to stay with Labor as the seat incorporates the City of Logan, and as such, is full of logans.

## Ryan QLD.

Sitting Member: **Jane Prentice (Liberal National)**

Margin: 8.98%

Profile: Jane Prentice first won pre-selection for this seat in 2010, after neglecting to tell the Liberal Party that she was a woman. The ruse ran for eight years until 2018 when the party finally discovered her gender, and immediately replaced her with new candidate Julian Simmonds.

## Wide Bay QLD.

Sitting Member: **Liew O'Brien (Liberal National)**

Margin: 8.19%

Profile: This electorate was originally going to be called Wide Berth until the naming committee, in its infinite wisdom, decided to steer clear of that name.

## Wright QLD.

Sitting Member: **Scott Buchholz (Liberal National)**

Margin: 9.69%

Profile: Scott Buchholz was once a staff member for Barnaby Joyce. He is pregnant with Barnaby's sixth child.

# SOUTH AUSTRALIA

## Adelaide S.A.

Sitting Member: **Kate Ellis (Labor) - retiring**

Margin: 8.30%

Profile: In 2008 Kate Ellis was named 'Australia's sexiest MP' by the Courier Mail. Luckily sexism in politics has since been eradicated.

## Barker S.A.

Sitting Member: **Tony Pasin (Liberal)**

Margin: Not telling

Profile: The electorate of Barker is named after Captain Collett Barker, whose claim to fame was being the first European, and the 128,156th person, to discover the mouth of the Murray River.

I'm voting Shooters and Fishers Party because I'm sick of our nanny state trampling on my right to be ruthlessly gunned down in a mass shooting
BILL HUNTER
MASOCHIST
SHOOTERS and FISHERS
SHOOTERS AND FISHERS PARTY
Not actually running in this election

## Boothby S.A.

Sitting Member: **Nicolle Flint (Liberal)**

Margin: 2.71%

Profile: Nicolle Flint has, on several occasions, called for the great white shark to be culled. Sure, he fluffed a few chances at the US Masters in the 1980s, but Jesus! Culling seems a bit extreme.

## Grey S.A.

Sitting Member: **Rowan Ramsey (Liberal)**

Margin: It's a secret

Profile: Grey, which covers 92% of South Australia, takes its name from the colour of the original sitting member's hair, after he had finally visited the entire electorate. He started when he was 18.

## Hindmarsh S.A.

Sitting Member: **Steve Georganas (Labor)**

Margin: 8.43

Profile: The government has committed over $4 billion to the construction of subs in this electorate, which is expected to create over 500 sandwich artist jobs in the region.

## Kingston S.A.

Sitting Member: **Amanda Rishworth (Labor)**

Margin: 13.55%

Profile: Amanda Rishworth is a former psychologist. She's more than happy to discuss the issues faced by voters in Kingston – it's just $180 for an initial one-hour consult.

## Makin S.A.

Sitting Member: **Tony Zappia (Labor)**

Margin: 10.79%

Profile: Tony Zappia is a ten-time champion powerlifter. According to Joe Hockey, many of the residents in Makin are powerleaners.

## Mayo S.A.

Sitting Member: **Rebekha Sharkie**

Margin: 5.3%

Profile: Until recently a blue-ribbon Liberal seat, Mayo was perceived as being too up itself, so changed its name from the original 'Aioli' to appear more relaxed and 'with it'.

## Spence S.A.

Sitting Member: **Nick Champion (notionally)**

Margin: 17.17%

Profile: This electorate, centred around the northern Adelaide suburb of Elizabeth, is named after Queen Elizabeth II, and shares all of her class. The Queen visited the area in 1963, sharing a few bongs with the locals before doing some max doeys in the royal carriage and fanging it back to the city.

## Did you know?

The former seat of Port Adelaide used to be the safest Labor seat in South Australia.

It was also the most dangerous Labor seat in South Australia.

# Sturt S.A.

Sitting member: **Christopher Pyne (Liberal) - Retiring**

Main opponent: **Christopher's twitter likes**

SANDSTONE BLUESTONE

26 years ago, the residents of this quiet, leafy inner-Adelaide electorate got so bored they voted in Christopher Pyne, just for something to do. They were then so appalled with their own actions, so filled with self-loathing, that they punished themselves by electing Christopher Pyne again in 1996. In a self-fulfilling cycle of personal flagellation and self-hatred, they have voted him into Parliament every three years since.

With Christopher Pyne announcing his retirement this year (he said he wanted to spend more time acting like a child) the residents of Burnside, Fullarton, Payneham, and Magill will need to find other ways to punish themselves.

***Did you know?** Christopher Pyne was just 25 years old when he entered Parliament. He's now eight.*

**6** number of seconds before someone in this electorate will ask you what school you went to

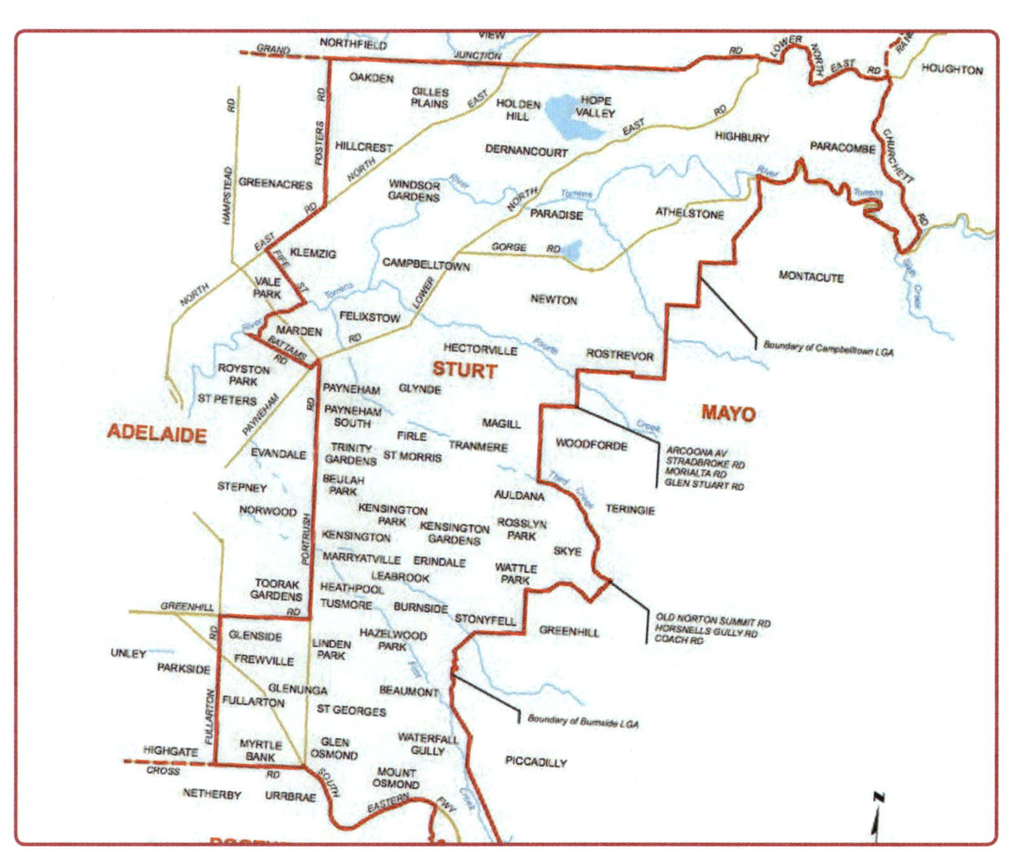

# Bass TAS.

Sitting member: **Ross Hart (Labor)**
Main opponent: **Tuna**

Voters in this northern Tasmanian electorate can be split neatly into three groups. People who cut down old-growth forests, people who chain themselves to old-growth forests, and people who remove people who are chained to old growth forests.

Or, to look at it in an economic context: the private sector, the unemployed and the public sector.

Or to look at it in a political context: Liberal voters, Greens voters, and Labor voters.

At the last election, people who remove people who are chained to old growth forests won the day, with 40% of the primary vote – giving Ross Hart his first victory.

People who chain themselves to old growth forests made up just 10% of the primary vote, a long way back from their high of almost 16% in 2010.

It is unclear whether these people have shifted to the side of the people who remove people who are chained to old-growth forests, or whether they just thought fuck it, let's chop these things down and be done with it. And anyway, there's something rather special about filling your printer with paper made from a tree that's been around since the 1700s.

Who will win this year? As a classic bellwether seat Bass is likely to be won by the party that wins overall/offers the biggest bribe.

Interestingly, the term 'bellwether' is derived from the practice of placing a bell around the neck of a castrated ram – a 'wether' – that leads a flock of sheep. No link really to this electorate, but still, an interesting way to end a profile, you'd have to admit.

***Did you know?** George Bass and Matthew Flinders were the first people to draw a map of Tasmania. It was at a life-drawing class in Darlinghurst.*

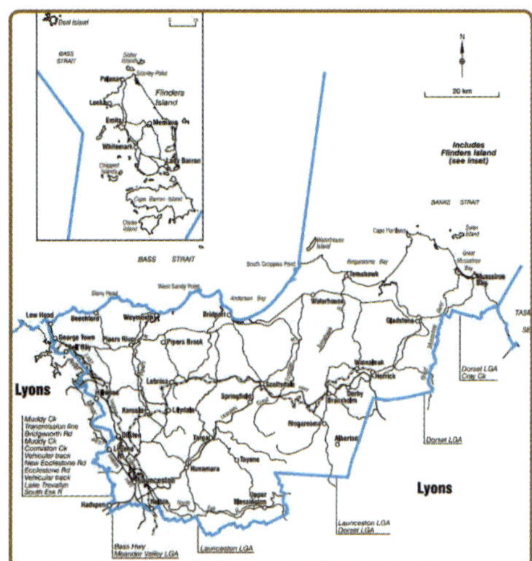

# TASMANIA

## Bass TAS.

Sitting Member: **Ross Hart (Liberal)**

Margin: 5.4%

Profile: Bass is named after George Bass, an 18th century gay maritime explorer. Bass Strait - the body of water separating Tasmania from mainland Australia - was named in his honour. Bass Gay wasn't deemed socially appropriate at the time.

## Braddon TAS.

Sitting Member: **Justine Keay (Labor)**

Margin: 1.73%

Profile: The seat of Braddon was named Darwin until 1955, when Tasmanians finally caught up on the news that the name was already taken.

## Clark (Formerly Denison) TAS.

Sitting Member: **Andrew Wilkie (Independent)**

Margin: 1 inch give or take

Profile: Independent Andrew Wilkie is going to have one more go at getting his pokie machine legislation through. Just one more go he promises, and then he's walking away. This is definitely the last go.

## Franklin TAS.

Sitting Member: **Julie Collins (Labor)**

Margin: 10.73%

Profile: Sick and tired of incest and 'two-head' jokes, Tasmanians have worked hard to transform their reputation in recent years by opening a museum that has a real life poo-making machine.

## Lyons TAS.

Sitting Member: **Brian Mitchell (Labor)**

Margin: 3.83%

Profile: In 2017 Brian Mitchell was accused of shouting at a journalist "go and do your research, maggot!". He claimed he had said "go and do your research, Matt". Interestingly, most AFL football umpires are also called Matt.

## Minor Party Profile:
## 60 Seconds with The Mature Australia Party

**Q: Who's hotter, Shorten or Morrison?**

A: Oh, what a childish way to start an interview.

**Q: Snapchat or Instagram?**

A: How trivial. Neither.

**Q: Who's your favourite Simpson's character?**

A: Really? Can we stick to politics please?

**Q: Should minor parties have to be accompanied by an adult?**

A: Oh please, what an immature joke.

**Q: How funny would it be if Scott Morrison accidentally called for an erection instead of an election?**

A: I think we'll end it there.

A FACE
YOU KNOW
AND TRUST.
Australian
Labor

I'm voting for the Smokers Rights Party because it's my right to decide what I KuRGHUGHugkHF, kUGH HEgK KuHG, HuKgHkhhh.
JOHN MARLBOROUGH
1983-2019
SMOKERS RIGHTS PARTY
We're really cool

# On the campaign trail with Dr Richard Di Natale

By James Jericho, Cadet Reporter for The Shovel

We're 158km north-east of Melbourne on the highway towards Albury, and Richard Di Natale – leader of The Greens – has a flat. Sleeves rolled up, and with a spring in his step, he goes about fixing it himself. He's nothing if not hands on.

It's a minor hiccup in what has otherwise been a successful morning on the campaign trail. We've covered more than eight kilometres already today and it's only 11am. Slow going some would say. But then, conducting an entire election campaign on a Black Pearl RD-140 pushbike is not without its challenges.

I'll be honest, driving alongside Richard Di Natale in a Prius while he cycled from electorate to electorate was not what I had imagined when I dreamed of becoming a political journalist. But with the current state of the media industry, you take what you can get. And anyway, it's given me a chance to see parts of this very specific part of north-eastern Victoria that I never knew existed.

"It's about reducing the carbon footprint," Di Natale reminds me, as he slips the bicycle tyre repair kit back into his pocket and reaches for the pump.

"I mean, the carbon emissions that Morrison and Shorten will generate as they crisscross the nation by plane is enormous. It's a joke. It's totally irresponsible".

He estimates the two party leaders will travel more than 40,000 km between them over the course of the campaign. Three weeks in, and we've come 284 km since we left Di Natale's Otways property. 298km if you count the day we had to backtrack, chasing after an empty plastic water bottle as it blew away from us in the wind.

It is, as Di Natale says, 'grassroots campaigning'. "We've had a chance to speak directly to dozens of potential Greens voters. And it's only day 23" he enthuses, as we pull back onto the highway.

Potential Greens voters like Bob McGuven who we met at the local pub in Euroa last night. A sheep farmer, Bob's voted Liberal all his life, but Di Natale thinks he may have a swinging voter on his hands.

"Bob and I chatted one-on-one for two hours last night, and he really warmed to the Greens position. You see, once you talk to people you have a chance to explain the issues to them. I've pencilled Bob's vote in".

Later I call Bob to verify some details for this story. "What did you think of Richard?" I ask.

"A lovely bloke, and generous too. Not at all what you'd expect from a politician," Bob says.

"Will you vote for him?"

"Not a fucking chance".

As we pass Violet Town, population 1,084, it seems as if Di Natale's puncture may be more serious than first thought. One of the spokes seems to be bent, which is affecting the steering. But Di Natale is determined to carry on. This is an important election campaign, he reminds me.

And anyway, Di Natale's staffer Sally Wales (who's made the journey by bike as well) is determined to make it to the electorate of Fenner in the ACT by next week. The Greens have a chance to improve their vote there, she says, and time on the ground could make all the difference.

We push on, singing 99 bottles hanging on the wall (but replaced with the words '499km, until we get to Fenner'), to keep our spirits up. Di Natale provides regular updates on how many tonnes of carbon

UPHILL BATTLE Being on a bike, Greens Leader finds going up-hill particularly hard.

we've saved, using the Carbon Saving app on his phone.

Two hours and 17 km later, at Wales's insistence, we stop. She says she's got something important to tell us. "Just got new polling results in," she announces, holding up her phone.

"Good news bad news.

"Bad news is, Fenner is a lost cause – no way we'll win there now. But the good news is Wannon in western Victoria is now in play". She gets back on her bike, turns around a starts cycling in the opposite direction, gesturing for us to follow.

I'm speechless. Wannon is 400km in the opposite direction. "Ah well," Di Natale says, gently smiling as he rides past the Prius. "That's politics!" He rings his bell, and pulls out back onto the road.

Back in Euroa, and things with Di Natale's bike have gone from bad to worse. We diagnose that the problem is actually now with the fork. It's been bent out of shape, and it'll need replacing if we're to get to Wannon before the election.

Wales makes some calls to bike shops in the area, but it's quite a specific part, and none have it on hand. Eventually she finds a shop in Shepparton that can send the part down to Euroa the following day. We spend the night in Euroa again, and catch up with Bob McGuven again for a beer.

The bike part doesn't arrive the following day, or the day after that. But Di Natale remains chipper. By day three he knows most people in the town by name.

"Well at least we can count on the vote in Euroa!" Di Natale says to a group of local farmers on the fourth night. There's an awkward murmur. Bob and I look down at our beers.

On our fifth day in Euroa, Wales gets a phone call from the bike shop in Shepparton.

"Good news bad news," she tells us. "The part's arrived, which is great."

"Fantastic!" Di Natale says. "So what's the bad news?"

"They had to fly it in from Denmark," she mumbles quickly.

"What?" Di Natale says.

"They had to fly the part in from a specialist factory in Copenhagen, Denmark," Wales says, still avoiding eye contact.

There's a prolonged silence. Then I accidentally say aloud, "Shall we check the Carbon Counter app?"

"Just leave it," Wales says.

Di Natale walks slowly out of the pub. He doesn't talk for the rest of the day.

The following week is less jovial than the previous few. The optimism is still there, but you sense the edge has been taken off.

There are some highlights – we bump into Scott Morrison who's on a fly-in fly-out campaign visit to Seymour. And Di Natale eventually comforts himself with the fact that – notwithstanding the spare part being flown in from northern Europe, and despite the fact that I accidentally had the Prius on high-performance petrol mode the whole time – we've still come in at well under the carbon miles of the two major party leaders. Which is, as Di Natale points out, a good news story for the media.

In the end, we do make it to Wannon. But unfortunately by then the polls are saying it's a lost cause for The Greens. On the plus side, there's been a spike in support up in northern NSW. Di Natale and Wales make plans to head there, but I won't be travelling with them. I've been assigned to follow the Love Australia or Leave party for the final weeks of the campaign.

On my last day on the trail we head to the pub for a farewell meal. The news is playing on the pub TV, and – as luck would have it – there's a story about the relative carbon footprints of each of the leaders' campaigns. According to the graphic, Di Natale's footprint is strangely much bigger than the other two leaders.

A voiceover explains the unexpected result. "Morrison and Shorten have cleverly bought carbon offsets this election year to bring their net carbon footprint down to zero".

Di Natale looks at his tattered bike, propped up next to the bar, then over to Wales. "Fuck. If only we'd thought of that".

# OUR PLAN FOR OUR FIRST 100 DAYS IN GOVERNMENT

## WE WILL: DISAPPOINT SALLY MCMANUS

From election night on, we promise to deliver a fraction of what our union paymasters want us to.

Unions are part of the Labor party, in that they pick up the bills and come to all our fundraisers, and so Labor promises to pay lip service to the unions on all the issues they care about.

If elected, we will copy and paste the Liberal Party's IR legislation and then insert the word "fair" into the title which will be the entirety of what unions have bought. Luckily, all union leaders have their eye on a cushy seat in parliament one day, so they will hail it as a massive win for the movement.

Bill Shorten will personally thank the unions in his acceptance speech, which is the last time he'll mention unions for the next two and a half years, until he needs the campaign cash again.

When he was at the Australian Workers' Union, Bill Shorten did deals with employers to deliver pay cuts to working Australians. We promise to deliver for workers as much as the AWU under Shorten delivered for workers.

## WE WILL: FAIL TO STOP ADANI

Policy details: The Adani mine, if it goes ahead, poses a threat to the future of the planet. Australia and the planet will be unable to meet its 2030 targets to reduce carbon output.

That said, existing environmental law is unable to be changed ever, and it is our long-held position that no government should ever promise to change a law on environmental grounds, because then donations from the CFMMEU would dry up.

Before the election, we committed to doing everything in our power to appear like we were doing everything in our power to appear like we were committed to stopping Adani. In the first 100 days, we will drop this pretence.

## WE WILL: BRING THE COUNTRY TOGETHER (AGAINST THE REFUGEES)

Bill Shorten promises to personally demonise each and every refugee in his election night acceptance speech. This is to unite all Australians together, especially the all-important "white racists" demographic, and reassure the nation during a change of government that nothing has changed except the brand name of the party running the country.

Then, in the first 100 days, Labor will Introduce a policy that Tony Abbott first came up with, but which, now five years later, seems "moderate" compared to the level of cruelty the Libs are currently hawking.

## WE WILL: STRIP UP TO 23 CENTS FROM RICH SCHOOLS OVER 10 YEARS

Billions of dollars are wasted each year funding private schools that don't need taxpayer support. In the first 100 days, the Labor Party will do jack shit to change this.

We will introduce a model of funding, based on the Gonski model, that redistributes up to 23 cents from the private sector to the public school system over 10 years. That's an extra 2.3 cents per year to the public school system per year!

I'm voting Green this election because I'm a hardcore conservative, and electing a minor party that splits the progressive vote is the surest way to ensure no progress is ever made in this country
CELION STARCHILD
ACTUALLY A BANKER
THE GREENS
THE AUSTRALIAN GREENS
Seriously though guys, the bees are dying

# Tim Wilson Confirms That Election Ballot Paper Will Now Contain Option To Donate To Liberal Party

The new ballot papers were kindly printed by a relative of Tim's for only twice the regular price

Voters in the upcoming election will have the option to donate to the Liberal Party when they fill in their ballot paper, in an innovative new system devised by MP Tim Wilson.

Under the new process, the House of Representatives ballot paper will now include a pre-ticked box to make it easier for voters to donate. The reverse side of the ballot paper will have space for the voters' credit card details and other information.

Mr Wilson denied it was an abuse of the democratic process, saying people were free to un-tick the box if they wanted. "We're not forcing people to donate. Of course their vote won't be counted if the box isn't ticked – that's part of the new process. But it's totally up to each individual if they want to vote or not".

Mr Wilson said voters would now receive three pieces of paper when they arrived at the voting booth – a Senate ballot paper, a House of Representatives ballot paper, and a membership form for the Liberal Party.

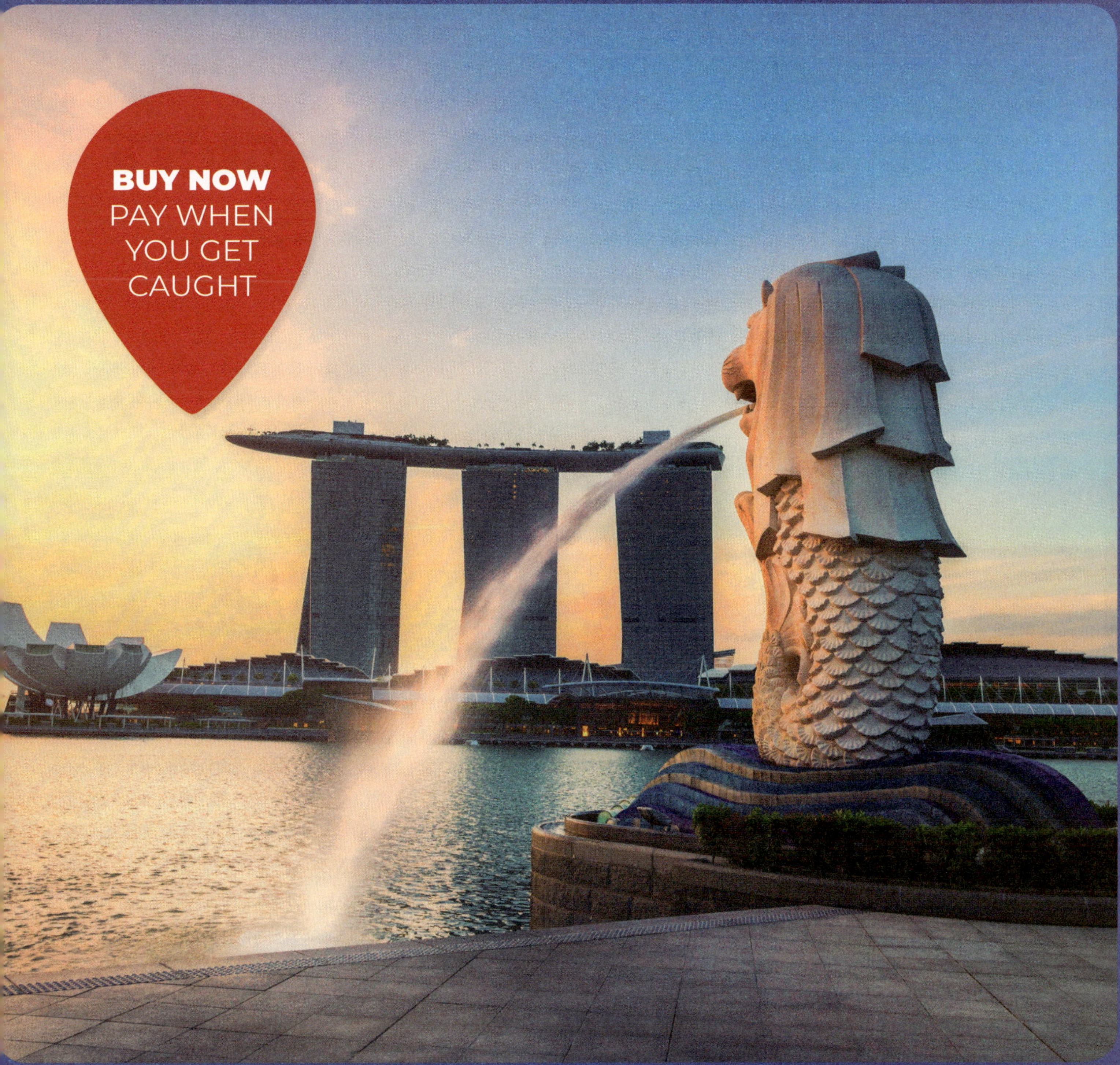
BUY NOW
PAY WHEN
YOU GET
CAUGHT

# HOLIDAY IN SINGAPORE

JUST **$0*** FOR A FAMILY OF FOUR!

TO BOOK, CALL OUR CEO DIRECT.
BECAUSE THAT'S TOTALLY NORMAL.

helloworld TRAVEL
THE TRAVEL PROFESSIONALS

*TERMS & CONDITIONS APPLY. ONLY AVAILABLE TO GOVERNMENT MINISTERS DURING THE PERIOD IN WHICH HELLOWORLD IS APPLYING FOR A $1 BILLION GOVERNMENT CONTRACT.

# The top 6 Prime Ministers of the last 2 years

It's a little known quirk of the Westminster System that the moment a sitting Prime Minister leaves the country, a fill-in takes over as Prime Minister until the real one returns. But what happens when the Deputy Prime Minister, who'd normally take over, is an omnishambles of a human, barely able to walk down the road without causing a national scandal? Well in that case things can get complicated and you may well end up with a few more Prime Ministers than you bargained for.

**MALCOLM TURNBULL**

*PM, 2015-2018*

Popularly known as the guy who slayed the onion eater, Malc takes out the number one spot for being the only Prime Minister of the six to actually be elected into the role.

**JULIE BISHOP**

*PM, OCT 2017*

Forced to take over when acting PM Barnaby Joyce was booted from Parliament for being a sheep shagger, Julie comes in at number two simply for not being Barnaby Joyce.

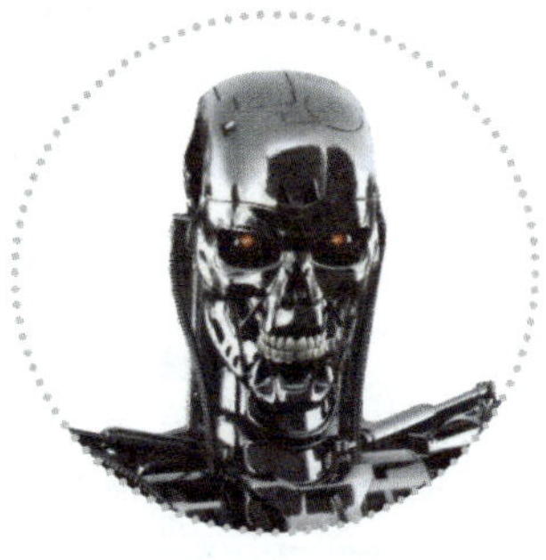

**MATIAS CORMANN**

*PM, FEB 2018*

Forced to step in to avoid Barnaby Joyce's pregnant mistress becoming first lady, Cormann comes in third for being the closest we'll get to having Arnie as Prime Minister.

**SCOTT MORRISON**

*PM, FROM AUG 2018*

Known for sculling beers and not catching buses, ScoMo comes in at number four, not because he's in any way a good PM, but rather because he's not Peter Dutton.

**MICHAEL MCCORMACK**

*PM, APR 2018*

Stepping into the role while Turnbull was overseas, Barnaby's replacement as Nationals leader was widely praised for his ability to refrain from sleeping with his staff while Turnbull was away.

**BARNABY JOYCE**

*PM, DEC 2017*

Temporarily slipping into the job between fuckups, December has now been declared a national month of mourning to commemorate the time we let this idiot become Prime Minister.

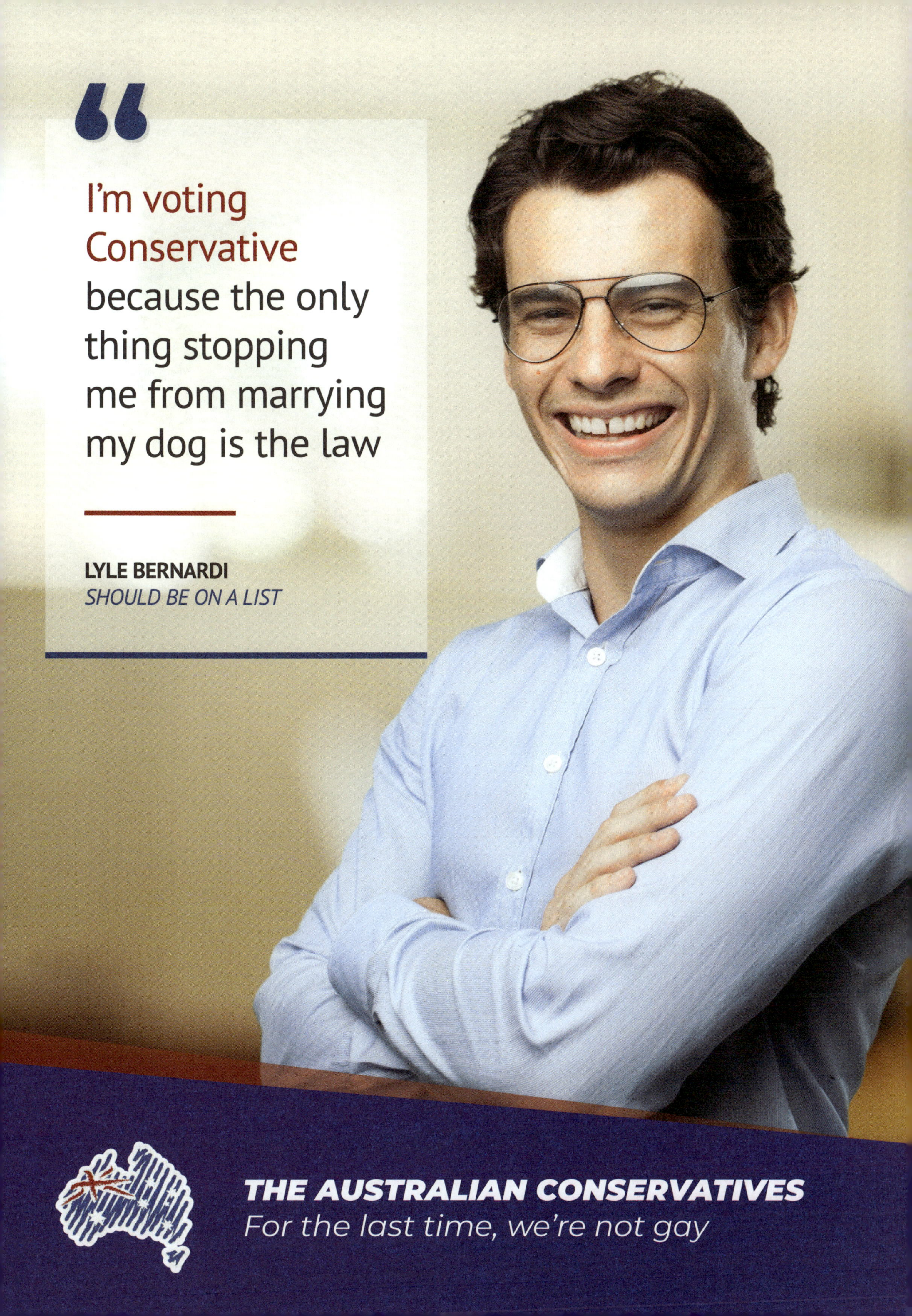

I'm voting Conservative because the only thing stopping me from marrying my dog is the law

**LYLE BERNARDI**
*SHOULD BE ON A LIST*

**THE AUSTRALIAN CONSERVATIVES**
*For the last time, we're not gay*

# APPLICATION TO JOIN THE LIBERAL PARTY

We've been accused of having a women problem in the Liberal Party. Not true. Three of our MPs are now women, which is 100% higher than the number of women at the private school we attended.

What's more, we have this special application form just for women. If you think your wife might be interested in the once-in-a-lifetime experience of standing in a safe Labor seat, please pass on this form. Don't forget to read over her work and sign at the bottom.

*Name:*

_______________

*Date of birth:*

_______________

*Favourite colour:*

_______________

*Dress size: (for your Liberal Party campaign T-shirt!)*

_______________

*Which all boys school did you attend:*

_______________

*Occupation: (of husband)*

_______________

*Name three men who inspire you:*

_______________

*How do you preferred to be bullied:*

_______________

*Give examples of your 'merit' (ie a list of your friends in the Liberal Party + business community):*

_______________

*Do you support quotas for women in parliament: (circle one)* [No] / [No]

*Signed* _______________

*Signed (husband or guardian):* _______________

# Leaked notes from the leadership debate

1/3

Economy
"I stopped the boats"

Health
"I stopped the boats"

Education
"I stopped the boats"
→ ~~Refugees are invading our schools~~??
→ MUSLIM EXTREMIST REFUGEE BOATS ARE INVADING OUR PRESCHOOLS ✓

HELLO!
my name is:
SCOMO
Prime Minister

3/3

Climate Change

♡ Coal ♡

Use notes from Minerals Council Fundraiser

- Marry coal?? Coal wedding?
- Love at first sight?
- "GBR is over rated anyway"

2/3

Refugees
"If elected I promise to personally murder anyone fleeing for their life from another ~~shithole~~ country"
✓✓✓ This tested well in focus groups.

Pedophiles
For? Against? Talk to Andrew Bolt
"Need a balanced approach"

REMEMBER:

* Pretend to be a human
* Blink at least once a minute

⟹ Establish trust with human beings

ECONOMY - I call for a royal commission into the economy

HEALTH - I call for a royal commission into hospitals

REFUGEES - I call for a royal commission into refugees

CLIMATE - I call for a royal commission into climate change
(Use notes from CFMMEU Mining fundraiser)

# The Micro Parties

It may to surprise you to learn that there are more than three parties running in the next federal election, in fact there are over 5! These other parties are called 'fucking dreaming' or, more formally, 'micro parties'. Micro parties tend to focus on a single issue, such as people being torn to shreds by crocodiles every month in North Queensland. However some micro parties, such as the Nationals, will put out an entire policy manifesto, despite the low likelihood they will ever get to see these policies put into action.

**THE SCIENCE PARTY**

The most boring party you'll ever go to. Say you're busy.

**TIM STORER INDEPENDENT PARTY**

The only party in Australia named after Tim Storer.

**PALMER UNITED PARTY**

A tiny party with an even smaller $1 billion marketing budget.

**SOCIALIST EQUALITY PARTY**

Believes everyone should be able to share equally in the depressing misery of socialism.

**BILL SHORTEN'S 21ST BIRTHDAY PARTY**

One of the smallest and least successful Australian parties of the post-war era.

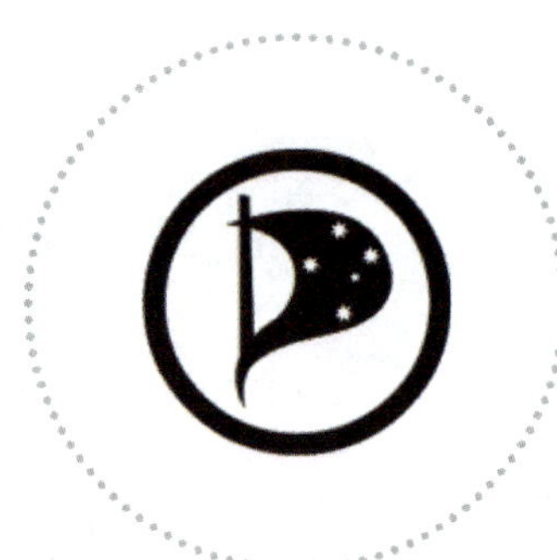

**PIRATE AUSTRALIA PARTY**

A small party started by Johnny Depp in a desperate attempt to save Pistol and Boo.

# The Micro Parties

### THE ANTI-VAXXER PARTY

Sadly forced to shut down after the party's website was infected with a virus in 2017. The party failed to install anti-virus software, fearing it may give the website autism.

### THE REASON PARTY

The Reason Party, formerly the Australian Sex Party, decided to change their name in 2016, reasoning they could do without the childish joke that brings in 99% of their votes.

### HEALTH AUSTRALIA PARTY

Believes in the power of naturopathy and natural healing to dramatically reduce the amount of money in Australians' wallets.

### CLIMATE ACTION! IMMIGRATION ACTION! ACCOUNTABLE POLITICIANS!

A single-issue party calling for mandatory exclamation marks at the end of every sentence.

### LOVE AUSTRALIA OR LEAVE PARTY

A party for people who believe Australia is no longer as good as it was during the White Australia policy. As a result, every member has now left Australia.

Logo courtesy of the 'Love MS Paint or Leave' Party

### HELP END MARIJUANA PROHIBITION (HEMP)

A single-issue party that wants to, ah that wants to ... shit dude, I can't remember. Fuck it. Doesn't matter.

# Election Glossary

*Do you get confused when politicians speak? Are you left wondering what they're really saying? To help you, we've translated into normal English a list of words and phrases used during an election campaign.*

## POLITICIANS

That's a great question, Leigh. I'm going to cut the ABC's budget immediately after I finish this interview.

That's a great question, Kochie. Your producer read my media release.

That's a great point, Alice. Somebody on my front bench has been back-grounding you and I'm going to tear their fucking throat out.

Can I just say...?. I didn't prep your question, so here's an answer to a question I prepared earlier.

I promise. I do not promise.

My team. Me.

Climate change. The second greatest challenge of our generation.

Party fundraising. The greatest challenge of our generation.

The science isn't settled. My party needs donations from coal companies.

Middle class. Working class.

Public transport. A worthy form of transport used by other people.

Roads. Votes.

Boats. Scary job-stealers.

Indigenous. I have a moral compass.

Good government. Bad government.

Short-term. One eight-hour news cycle.

Long-term. One day.

Generational. One week.

Negative gearing. The great Australian dream.

Superannuation. Tax avoidance scheme for everyone.

High speed rail. The infra-structure equivalent of a balanced budget.

Marriage equality. The National Party should get equal seats in cabinet.

Balanced budget. The budget equivalent of high-speed rail.

Budget surplus. Fucking GFC.

Cities. Sydney and Melbourne.

Rural and regional com-munities. Foreign-owned agribusinesses.

I don't pay much attention to the polls. Polls are literally the only thing I read.

Family values. My own family's values.

Balanced. A situation that appears whenever a policy wonk from a right wing think tank appears on The Bolt Report to discuss affairs with a Liberal National politician.

Core values. It's the most expedient option.

Consult. To pay lip service.

Queue jumper. Someone who hasn't read the UN Guide to the Etiquette of People Fleeing Harm and Conflict.

Reality check. Poll numbers.

Rural values. Interchange-able with family values, but with flies and cow shit.

Silver bullet. Something that doesn't exist; also any policy announced during an election campaign.

Sustainable. We're going to leave something for our grand-kids to dig up, fell or burn.

Sustainable growth. Unsus-tainable growth.

Crunch time. I'm about to be rolled.

Budget update. Announc-ing the numbers that we decided to hide from you six months ago.

Vision. A projected ideal situation that will not be seen around here any time soon; but nevertheless, much lauded; a rare commodity (see megafauna or golden geese).

## JOURNALISTS

Critics say. I say.

I'll take that as a comment. Thanks, nutter.

The report says. I haven't read the report, but I've read the Twitter summary.